26 ✔ KU-720-701

CHARLESTON ACADEMY
ENGLISH DEPARTMENT

JOURNEY'S END

A realistic picture of life in a front-line trench in the First World War, which makes a very powerful impression on the stage.

THE HEREFORD PLAYS

General Editor: E. R. Wood

Maxwell Anderson
Winterset

Robert Ardrey
Thunder Rock

Robert Bolt
A Man for All Seasons
The Tiger and the
* Horse*
Vivat! Vivat Regina!

Harold Brighouse
Hobson's Choice

Coxe and Chapman
Billy Budd

Gordon Daviot
Dickon

Barry England
Conduct Unbecoming

J. E. Flecker
Hassan

Ruth and Augustus
Goetz
The Heiress

H. Granville-Barker
The Voysey Inheritance

(Ed.) E. Haddon
Three Dramatic
* Legends*

Willis Hall
The Long and the Short
* and the Tall*

Fritz Hochwälder
The Strong are Lonely

Henrik Ibsen
The Master Builder
An Enemy of the People

D.H. Lawrence
The Widowing of Mrs
* Holroyd and The*
* Daughter-in-Law*

Roger MacDougall
Escapade

Arthur Miller
The Crucible
Death of a Salesman
All My Sons

André Obey
Noah

J. B. Priestley
An Inspector Calls
Time and the Conways
When We are Married
Eden End

James Saunders
Next Time I'll Sing to
* You*
A Scent of Flowers

R. C. Sherriff
Journey's End

David Storey
In Celebration

J. M. Synge
The Playboy of the
* Western World and*
* Riders to the Sea*

Brandon Thomas
Charley's Aunt

Peter Ustinov
Romanoff and Juliet

John Whiting
Marching Song
Saint's Day
A Penny for a Song
The Devils

Oscar Wilde
The Importance of
* Being Earnest*

Tennessee Williams
The Glass Menagerie

R. C. Sherriff

Journey's End

with an *Introduction* **and** *Notes by*

E. R. WOOD

HEINEMANN EDUCATIONAL BOOKS
LONDON

Heinemann Educational Books Ltd

LONDON EDINBURGH MELBOURNE AUCKLAND TORONTO
HONG KONG SINGAPORE KUALA LUMPUR NEW DELHI
NAIROBI JOHANNESBURG LUSAKA IBADAN
KINGSTON

ISBN 0 435 22800 5

Journey's End—Copyright R. C. Sherriff 1929
Introduction and Questions to this Edition of *Journey's End*
© E. R. Wood 1958

First published 1929
First Educational Edition 1958
Reprinted 1961, 1962, 1963, 1965, 1966, 1967, 1968, 1970, 1972,
1973, 1974, 1976, 1978

**All rights whatsoever in this play are strictly reserved and
applications for permission to perform it must be made by
amateur companies to Samuel French Ltd, 26 Southampton
Street, London, W.C.2, and professional companies to Curtis
Brown Academic, 1 Craven Hill, London W2 3EP**

Published by
Heinemann Educational Books Ltd
48 Charles Street, London W1X 8AH
Printed in Great Britain for the Publishers by
Cox & Wyman Ltd, London, Fakenham and Reading

Contents

R. C. SHERRIFF

R. C. SHERRIFF was born in 1896 and educated at Kingston Grammar School and New College, Oxford. He served as a Captain in the East Surrey Regiment. When he wrote *Journey's End* he was working in an insurance office. The play brought him wealth and fame.

Among his other plays are *Badger's Green* (1930), a delightful comedy of village people preoccupied with cricket; *Windfall* (1933); *St. Helena* (1935), a play about Napoleon, written in collaboration with Jeanne de Casalis; *Miss Mabel* (1948); *Home at Seven* (1950); *The White Carnation* (1953); and *The Long Sunset* (1955), a vivid picture of the last days of Roman civilisation in Britain. His most recent play is *The Telescope*.

He wrote screen plays for the following films: *The Invisible Man* (1933), *Goodbye, Mr. Chips* (1933), *The Four Feathers* (1938), *Lady Hamilton* (1941), *Odd Man Out* (1945), *Quartet* (1948), *No Highway* (1950), *The Dam Busters* (1955).

Introduction

by E. R. Wood

THE first performance of *Journey's End* was the prelude to an immense stage success. The play had previously been rejected by most of the theatre managements in London; some thought that the public did not want to hear about war, others that a play without women would not be popular. At last it was given a single Sunday evening performance by the Incorporated Stage Society in December, 1928. Laurence Olivier, then only twenty-one years old, played Stanhope on that occasion. In the audience was an actor, Maurice Browne, who recognised the play's quality and undertook to produce it at the Savoy Theatre, where it ran for two years. Everyone who saw it must remember still the profound impression it made. Its young author, hitherto unknown, was suddenly famous; the play was translated into every European language and performed all over the world. Although R. C. Sherriff has since written several other successful plays, a few novels, and screen plays for some of the best-known films of our time, his name is still most widely associated with his first great triumph, *Journey's End*.

Looking back over the years, it is surprising only that the play's theatrical possibilities were ever doubted. It has obvious qualities which should have commended it to theatre people: a handful of excellent acting parts; a series of highly dramatic scenes, with a salting of ironic comedy, culminating in a shattering climax; a realistic atmosphere created by convincing detail and natural dialogue. Moreover, it is completely comprehensible at a first hearing; unlike many modern plays, it does not require its audience to follow subtle clues to meaning or to respond to delicate refinements of emotion; there is nothing " highbrow " in its language, its ideas or its conception of personality. Such qualities should have ensured at least a moderately warm reception from theatre managements. Once given its chance, it could not fail. But in order to understand the overwhelming impact that it made, we must look at the spirit of the time.

The first World War had ended ten years before. Ten million men had been killed, the majority of them in the maze of trenches which stretched across Europe from Switzerland to

the North Sea. For four years the huge armies had been bogged
down in the mud of Flanders, each side massing men and guns
from time to time for a mighty effort to break through, usually
pushing a few miles for the loss of hundreds of thousands of
men, only to be pushed back again by the next big offensive of
the enemy. The mood of heroic optimism in which the British
had first entered the fight gradually changed to disillusion and
bitterness. When at last the war was over, men who had lived
through the bloodshed and misery wanted at first to forget.
In 1928, ten years later, they could bear to look back on the
world crisis, which had, of course, been a momentous experience
for them, a time when a man's quality was put to the test,
when comradeship and fortitude mattered more than in peace-
time. These ex-soldiers would have scoffed, however, at any
glorified picture of war as a noble contest, directed by all-wise
generals and waged by romantic heroes, as imagined by people
who had never seen the real thing. R. C. Sherriff had been a
soldier, and his portrayal of trench warfare was recognised as
authentic by those who knew.

Most of the people who crowded to see the play had never,
of course, been in a front-line trench. But the general public,
too, were in tune with the mood of *Journey's End*. After the
victory of 1918 there had been a period of easy optimism, when
there was talk of having won " a War to end Wars " and of
building " a land fit for heroes to live in." By 1928 the world
was disillusioned; the peace had not proved sweet and seemed
unlikely to be permanent. People were ready to be shown the
grim truth about war and were deeply moved as it was brought
home to them so uncompromisingly. Some saw in the play a
message of support for Peace organisations. On the other hand,
men who despised pacifist talk and admired the military virtues
above all others could also find encouragement in the play,
which does show ordinary men doing their duty and " sticking
it because it's the only decent thing a man can do." Thus the
play spoke to many kinds of people, both ex-soldier and civilian,
patriot and internationalist, young and old; to people of all
nations, including those who had been our enemies.

If you look at a list of plays that were enjoying long runs
thirty years ago, you will find that most of them are forgotten
today. In particular those which owed much of their original
success to striking the mood of their time (like Noël Coward's
The Vortex or *Easy Virtue*) appear all the more out-dated a

generation later. This has not happened to *Journey's End*. After another world conflict and an uneasy post-war decade in the shadow of nuclear explosions, it is surprising to find that *Journey's End* has suffered so little. Of course it does bear a few marks of time. Some of the slang of an earlier generation (" simply topping," " jolly bucked," " thanks most awfully ") sounds a little embarrassing today, but in general the dialogue has not dated enough to matter. There is a suggestion of class-consciousness—an implication that our natural leaders come from the public schools, while the rest, though they may be good fellows in their way, appropriately provide the comic element in a play. The English are still very sensitive to differences of social class, but since the second World War, with its reliance for leadership on a wider section of our society, the soldierly virtues are less definitely associated with the playing-fields of the most exclusive schools.

Apart from these minor changes, the play is still very much alive. The second World War was very different from the first; the prolonged carnage in static lines of trenches and dug-outs was not repeated. Yet to the soldiers of 1939–45 the dug-out near St. Quentin seems familiar enough; the grimly realistic view of war is as telling as ever. That incident in Flanders on a March evening in 1918 now takes on something of the eternal. We may even find in Shakespeare's *Henry V* a number of soldiers who would not have looked out of place in the British trenches before St. Quentin. Perhaps soldiers in hardship and danger were always much the same, ready to give all their fame for a pot of ale and safety; prone to joke in the grimmest crises and to speak of the familiar enemy without hate; sceptical about military orders from above, but still carrying them out. The soldiers of *Journey's End* are of all time.

Greek Tragedy was concerned with the spectacle of Man pitted against a harsh and unrelenting Fate. So are Stanhope and his men, involved in a world catastrophe that is not of their making—a kind of huge machine that is out of human control. They have no choice, it seems, but to keep the war going, to do their duty or despise themselves while others do it for them. Senseless though their struggle seems, it has its touches of nobility. Sherriff's view of it is distinguished by its honesty, its understanding and its deep compassion. Without such greater qualities it would not have caught and kept the ear of different generations and people of all nations.

CHARACTERS

STANHOPE, Commanding an Infantry Company
OSBORNE ⎫
TROTTER ⎪
HIBBERT ⎬ Officers of the Company
RALEIGH ⎭
THE COLONEL
THE COMPANY SERGEANT-MAJOR
MASON, the Officers' Cook
HARDY, an Officer of another Regiment
A YOUNG GERMAN SOLDIER
TWO PRIVATE SOLDIERS OF THE COMPANY

Journey's End was first produced by the Incorporated Stage Society at the Apollo Theatre, London, on 9th December 1928, with the following cast:

STANHOPE	Laurence Olivier
OSBORNE	George Zucco
TROTTER	Melville Cooper
HIBBERT	Robert Speaight
RALEIGH	Maurice Evans
THE COLONEL	H. G. Stoker
THE COMPANY SERGEANT-MAJOR	Percy Walsh
MASON	Alexander Field
HARDY	David Horne
GERMAN SOLDIER	Geoffrey Wincott

The Play Produced by JAMES WHALE

Subsequently the play was presented by Maurice Browne at the Savoy Theatre on 21st January 1929.

THE SCENE

A dug-out in the British trenches before St. Quentin.

*A few rough steps lead into the trench above, through a low doorway.
A table occupies a good space of the dug-out floor. A wooden frame,
covered with wire netting, stands against the left wall and serves the
double purpose of a bed and a seat for the table. A wooden bench
against the back wall makes another seat, and two boxes serve for
the other sides.*

Another wire-covered bed is fixed in the right corner beyond the doorway.

Gloomy tunnels lead out of the dug-out to left and right.

*Except for the table, beds, and seats, there is no furniture save the
bottles holding the candles, and a few tattered magazine pictures
pinned to the wall of girls in flimsy costumes.*

*The earth walls deaden the sounds of war, making them faint and far
away, although the front line is only fifty yards ahead. The flames of
the candles that burn day and night are steady in the still, damp air.*

ACT I
Evening on Monday, the 18th March 1918

ACT II
SCENE 1: Tuesday morning.

SCENE 2: Tuesday afternoon.

ACT III
SCENE 1: Wednesday afternoon.

SCENE 2: Wednesday night.

SCENE 3: Thursday, towards dawn.

ACT I

The evening of a March day. A pale glimmer of moonlight shines down the narrow steps into one corner of the dug-out. Warm yellow candle-flames light the other corner from the necks of two bottles on the table. Through the doorway can be seen the misty grey parapet of a trench and a narrow strip of starlit sky. A bottle of whisky, a jar of water, and a mug stand on the table amongst a litter of papers and magazines. An officer's equipment hangs in a jumbled mass from a nail in the wall.

CAPTAIN HARDY, a red-faced, cheerful-looking man, is sitting on a box by the table, intently drying a sock over a candle-flame. He wears a heavy trench-boot on his left leg, and his right foot, which is naked, is held above the damp floor by resting it on his left knee. His right boot stands on the floor beside him. As he carefully turns the sock this way and that—feeling it against his face to see if it is dry—he half sings, half hums a song—humming when he is not quite sure of the words, and marking time with the toes of his right foot.

HARDY: One and Two, it's with Maud and Lou;
         Three and Four, two girls more;
         Five and Six it's with—hm—hm—hm—
         Seven, Eight, Clara and Caroline—

He lapses into an indefinite humming, and finishes with a lively burst:
         Tick!—Tock!—wind up the clock,
         And we'll start the day over again.

A man's legs appear in the moonlit trench above, and a tall, thin man comes slowly down the dug-out steps, stooping low to avoid the roof. He takes his helmet off and reveals a fine head, with close-cropped, iron-grey hair. He looks about forty-five—physically as hard as nails.

HARDY (*looking round*): Hullo, Osborne! Your fellows arriving?

OSBORNE (*hitching off his pack and dropping it in a corner*): Yes. They're just coming in.

HARDY: Splendid! Have a drink.

OSBORNE: Thanks. (*He crosses and sits on the left-hand bed.*)

HARDY (*passing the whisky and a mug*): Don't have too much water. It's rather strong today.

OSBORNE (*slowly mixing a drink*): I wonder what it *is* they put in the water.

HARDY: Some sort of disinfectant, I suppose.

OSBORNE: I'd rather have the microbes, wouldn't you?

HARDY: *I* would—yes——

OSBORNE: Well, cheero.

HARDY: Cheero.   Excuse my sock, won't you?

OSBORNE: Certainly.   It's a nice-looking sock.

HARDY: It is rather, isn't it?   Guaranteed to keep the feet dry. Trouble is, it gets so wet doing it.

OSBORNE: Stanhope asked me to come and take over.   He's looking after the men coming in.

HARDY: Splendid!   You know, I'm awfully glad you've come.

OSBORNE: I heard it was a quiet bit of line up here.

HARDY: Well, yes—in a *way*.   But you never know.   Sometimes nothing happens for hours on end; then—all of a sudden— " over she comes! "—rifle grenades—Minnies[1]—and those horrid little things like pineapples—you know.

OSBORNE: I know.

HARDY: Swish—swish—swish—swish—BANG!

OSBORNE: All right—all right—I know.

HARDY: They simply blew us to bits yesterday.   Minnies— enormous ones; about twenty.   Three bang in the trench.   I really *am* glad you've come; I'm not simply being polite.

OSBORNE: Do much damage?

HARDY: Awful.   A dug-out got blown up and came down in the men's tea.   They were frightfully annoyed.

OSBORNE: I know.   There's nothing worse than dirt in your tea.

HARDY: By the way, you know the big German attack's expected any day now?

OSBORNE: It's been expected for the last month.

[1] Minnies—German gun known as *minenwerfer* or *minethrower*.

HARDY: Yes, but's it's very near now: there's funny things happening over in the Boche[1] country. I've been out listening at night when it's quiet. There's more transport than usual coming up—you can hear it rattling over the *pavé*[2] all night; more trains in the distance—puffing up and going away again, one after another, bringing up loads and loads of men——

OSBORNE: Yes. It's coming—pretty soon now.

HARDY: Are you here for six days?

OSBORNE: Yes.

HARDY: Then I should think you'll get it—right in the neck.

OSBORNE: Well, you won't be far away. Come along, let's do this handing over. Where's the map?

HARDY: Here we are. (*He gropes among the papers on the table and finds a tattered map.*) We hold about two hundred yards of front line. We've got a Lewis gun[3] just here—and one here, in this little sap.[4] Sentry posts where the crosses are——

OSBORNE: Where do the men sleep?

HARDY: *I* don't know. The sergeant-major sees to that. (*He points off to the left.*) The servants and signallers sleep in there. Two officers in here, and three in there. (*He points to the right-hand tunnel.*) That is, if you've *got* five officers.

OSBORNE: We've only got four at present, but a new man's coming up tonight. He arrived at transport lines a day or two ago.

HARDY: I hope you get better luck than I did with *my* last officer. He got lumbago the first night and went home. Now he's got a job lecturing young officers on " Life in the Front Line."

OSBORNE: Yes. They do send some funny people over here nowadays. I hope we're lucky and get a youngster straight from school. They're the kind that do best.

HARDY: I suppose they are, really.

OSBORNE: Five beds, you say? (*He examines the one he is sitting on.*) Is this the best one?

[1] Boche—German. [2] *pavé*—stone cobbled road.
[3] Lewis gun—type of machine gun.
[4] sap—a narrow trench projecting towards the enemy lines.

HARDY: Oh, no. (*He points to the bed in the right corner.*) *That's* mine. The ones in the other dug-out haven't got any bottoms to them. You keep yourself in by hanging your arms and legs over the sides. Mustn't hang your legs too low, or the rats gnaw your boots.

OSBORNE: You got many rats here?

HARDY: I should say—roughly—about two million; but then, of course, I don't see them all. (*He begins to put on his sock and draw on his boot.*) Well, there's nothing else you want to know, is there?

OSBORNE: You haven't told me anything yet.

HARDY: What else do you *want* to know?

OSBORNE: Well, what about trench stores?

HARDY: You *are* a fussy old man. Anybody'd think you were in the Army. (*He finds a tattered piece of paper.*) Here you are: 115 rifle grenades—I shouldn't use them if I were you; they upset Jerry[1] and make him offensive. Besides, they are rusty, in any case. Then there's 500 Mills bombs, 34 gum boots——

OSBORNE: That's seventeen pairs——

HARDY: Oh, no; 25 right leg and 9 left leg. But everything's down here. (*He hands the list to* OSBORNE.)

OSBORNE: Did you check it when you took over?

HARDY: No. I think the sergeant-major did. It's quite all right.

OSBORNE: I expect Stanhope would like to see you before you go. He always likes a word with the company commander he's relieving.

HARDY: How *is* the dear young boy? Drinking like a fish, as usual?

OSBORNE: Why do you say that?

HARDY: Well, damn it, it's just the natural thing to ask about Stanhope. (*He pauses, and looks curiously at* OSBORNE.) Poor old man. It must be pretty rotten for you, being his second in command, and you such a quiet, sober old thing.

OSBORNE: He's a long way the best company commander we've got.

[1] Jerry—familiar name for Germans.

HARDY: Oh, he's a good chap, I know. But I never *did* see a youngster put away the whisky he does. D'you know, the last time we were out resting at Valennes he came to supper with us and drank a whole bottle in one hour fourteen minutes—we timed him.

OSBORNE: I suppose it amused everybody; I suppose everybody cheered him on, and said what a splendid achievement it was.

HARDY: He didn't want any " cheering " on——

OSBORNE: No, but everybody thought it was a big thing to do. (*There is a pause.*) Didn't they?

HARDY: Well, you can't help, somehow, *admiring* a fellow who can do that—and then pick out his own hat all by himself and walk home——

OSBORNE: When a boy like Stanhope gets a reputation out here for drinking, he turns into a kind of freak show exhibit. People pay with a bottle of whisky for the morbid curiosity of seeing him drink it.

HARDY: Well, naturally, you're biased. You have to put him to bed when he gets home.

OSBORNE: It rather reminds you of bear-baiting—or cock-fighting—to sit and watch a boy drink himself unconscious.

HARDY: Well, damn it, it's pretty dull without *something* to liven people up. I mean, after all—Stanhope really *is* a sort of freak; I mean it *is* jolly fascinating to see a fellow drink like he does—glass after glass. He didn't go home on his last leave, did he?

OSBORNE: No.

HARDY: I suppose he didn't think he was fit to meet papa. (*A pause.*) You know his father's vicar of a country village?

OSBORNE: I know.

HARDY (*laughing*): Imagine Stanhope spending his leave in a country vicarage sipping tea! He spent his last leave in Paris, didn't he?

OSBORNE: Yes.

HARDY: I bet it was *some* leave!

OSBORNE: Do you know how long he's been out here?

HARDY: A good time, I know.

OSBORNE: Nearly three years. He came out straight from school—when he was eighteen. He's commanded this company for a year—in and out of the front line. He's never had a rest. Other men come over here and go home again ill, and young Stanhope goes on sticking it, month in, month out.

HARDY: Oh, I know he's a jolly good fellow——

OSBORNE: I've seen him on his back all day with trench fever—then on duty all night——

HARDY: Oh, I know; he's a splendid chap!

OSBORNE: And because he's stuck it till his nerves have got battered to bits, he's called a drunkard.

HARDY: Not a drunkard; just a—just a hard drinker; but you're quite right about his nerves. They *are* all to blazes. Last time out resting we were playing bridge and something happened—I don't remember what it was; some silly little argument—and all of a sudden he jumped up and knocked all the glasses off the table! Lost control of himself; and then he—sort of—came to—and cried——

OSBORNE: Yes, I know.

HARDY: You heard about it?

OSBORNE: He told me.

HARDY: Did he? We tried to hush it up. It just shows the state he's in. (*He rises and puts on his pack. There is a pause.*) You know, Osborne, *you* ought to be commanding this company.

OSBORNE: Rubbish!

HARDY: Of course you ought. It sticks out a mile. I know he's got pluck and all that, but, damn it, man, you're twice his age—and think what a dear, level-headed old thing you are.

OSBORNE: Don't be an ass. He was out here before I joined up. His experience alone makes him worth a dozen people like me.

HARDY: You know as well as I do, you ought to be in command.

OSBORNE: There isn't a man to touch him as a commander of men. He'll command the battalion one day if——

HARDY: Yes, if! (*He laughs.*)

OSBORNE: You don't know him as I do; I love that fellow. I'd go to hell with him.

HARDY: Oh, you sweet, sentimental old darling!

OSBORNE: Come along. Finish handing over and stop blithering.

HARDY: There's nothing else to do.

OSBORNE: What about the log-book?

HARDY: God! you are a worker. Oh, well. Here we are. (*He finds a tattered little book among the papers on the table.*) Written right up to date; here's my last entry: " 5 p.m. to 8 p.m. All quiet. German airman flew over trenches. Shot a rat."

OSBORNE: Did he?

HARDY: No, I shot the rat, you ass. Well, finish up your whisky. I want to pack my mug. I'll leave you that drop in the bottle.

OSBORNE: Thanks. (*He drinks up his whisky and hands* HARDY *the mug.*)

HARDY (*tucking the mug into his pack*): I'll be off.

OSBORNE: Aren't you going to wait and see Stanhope?

HARDY: Well, no, I don't specially want to see him. He's so fussy about the trenches. I expect they *are* rather dirty. He'll talk for hours if he catches me.

He hitches his pack over his shoulders, hangs on his gas satchel, map-case, binoculars, compass-case, until he looks like a travelling pedlar. (As he dresses.) Well, I hope you have a nice six days. Don't forget to change your clothes if you get wet.

OSBORNE: No, papa.

HARDY: And don't forget about the big attack.

OSBORNE: Oh, Lord, no, I mustn't miss that! I'll make a note in my diary.

HARDY (*fully dressed*): There we are! Do I look every inch a soldier?

OSBORNE: Yes. I should get quite a fright if I were a German and met you coming round a corner.

HARDY: I should bloody well hope you would.

OSBORNE: Shouldn't be able to run away for laughing.

HARDY: Now don't be rude. (*He leans over to light a cigarette from a candle, and looks down on the table.*) Well, I'm damned. Still at it!

OSBORNE: What is?

HARDY: Why, that earwig. It's been running round and round that candle since tea-time; must have done a mile.

OSBORNE: I shouldn't hang about here if I were an earwig.

HARDY: Nor should I. I'd go home. Ever had earwig races?

OSBORNE: No.

HARDY: Great fun. We've had 'em every evening.

OSBORNE: What are the rules?

HARDY: Oh, you each have an earwig, and start 'em in a line. On the word " Go " you dig your earwig in the ribs and steer him with a match across the table. I won ten francs last night—had a *splendid* earwig. I'll give you a tip.

OSBORNE: Yes?

HARDY: Promise not to let it go any farther?

OSBORNE: Yes.

HARDY: Well, if you want to get the best pace out of an earwig, dip it in whisky—makes 'em go like hell!

OSBORNE: Right. Thanks awfully.

HARDY: Well, I must be off. Cheero!

OSBORNE: Cheero!

HARDY *goes up the narrow steps into the trench above, singing softly and happily to himself:*

" One and Two, it's with Maud and Lou;
    Three and Four, two girls more——"

The words trail away into the night.

OSBORNE *rises and takes his pack from the floor to the bed by the table. While he undoes it a* SOLDIER SERVANT *comes out of the tunnel from the left with a table-cloth over his arm and a plate with half a loaf of bread on it.*

MASON: Excuse me, sir. Can I lay supper?

OSBORNE: Yes, do. (*He shuffles up the papers from the table and puts them on the bed.*)

MASON: Thank you, sir.   (*He lays the table.*)

OSBORNE: What are you going to tempt us with tonight, Mason?

MASON: Soup, sir—cutlets—and pineapple.

OSBORNE (*suspiciously*): Cutlets?

MASON: Well, sir—well, yes, sir—cutlets.

OSBORNE: What sort of cutlets?

MASON: Now, sir, you've got me. I shouldn't like to commit meself too deep, sir.

OSBORNE: Ordinary ration meat?

MASON: Yes, sir. Ordinary ration meat, but a noo shape, sir. Smells like liver, sir, but it 'asn't got that smooth, wet look that liver's got.

MASON *leaves the dug-out.*

OSBORNE *sits up to the table and examines the map. Voices come from the trench above; a gruff voice says:* " This is ' C ' Company 'Eadquarters, sir."

A boyish voice replies: " Oh, thanks."

There is a pause, then the gruff voice says: " Better go down, sir." *The boyish voice replies:* " Yes. Righto."

AN OFFICER *comes groping down the steps and stands in the candle-light. He looks round, a little bewildered. He is a well-built, healthy-looking boy of about eighteen, with the very new uniform of a 2nd lieutenant.*

OSBORNE *looks up from the trench map, surprised and interested to see a stranger.*

OSBORNE: Hullo!

RALEIGH: Good evening (*he notices* OSBORNE'S *grey hair and adds:*) sir.

OSBORNE: You the new officer?

RALEIGH: Er—yes. I've been to Battalion Headquarters. They told me to report here.

OSBORNE: Good. We've been expecting you. Sit down, won't you?

RALEIGH: Thanks.   (*He sits gingerly on the box opposite* OSBORNE.)

OSBORNE: I should take your pack off.

RALEIGH: Oh, right.   (*He slips his pack from his shoulders.*)

OSBORNE: Will you have a drink?

RALEIGH: Er—well——

OSBORNE: You don't drink whisky?

RALEIGH (*hastily*): Oh, yes—er—just a small one, sir.

OSBORNE (*pouring out a small whisky and adding water*): Whisky takes away the taste of the water——

RALEIGH: Oh, yes?   (*He pauses, and laughs nervously.*)

OSBORNE: —and the water takes away the taste of the whisky. (*He hands* RALEIGH *the drink.*) Just out from England?

RALEIGH: Yes, I landed a week ago.

OSBORNE: Boulogne?

RALEIGH: Yes.   (*A pause, then he self-consciously holds up his drink.*) Well, here's luck, sir.

OSBORNE (*taking a drink himself*): Good luck.   (*He takes out a cigarette case.*) Cigarette?

RALEIGH: Thanks.

OSBORNE (*holding a bottle across so that* RALEIGH *can light his cigarette from the candle in it*): Ever been up in the line before?

RALEIGH: Oh, no. You see, I only left school at the end of last summer term.

OSBORNE: I expect you find it a bit strange.

RALEIGH (*laughing*): Yes—I do—a bit——

OSBORNE: My name's Osborne. I'm second in command of the company. You only call me " sir " in front of the men.

RALEIGH: I see.   Thanks.

OSBORNE: You'll find the other officers call me " Uncle."

RALEIGH: Oh, yes?   (*He smiles.*)

OSBORNE: What's *your* name?

RALEIGH: Raleigh.

OSBORNE: I knew a Raleigh. A master at Rugby.

RALEIGH: Oh? He may be a relation. I don't know. I've got lots of uncles and—and things like that.

OSBORNE: We've only just moved into these trenches. Captain Stanhope commands the company.

RALEIGH (*suddenly brightening up*): I know. It's a frightful bit of luck.

OSBORNE: Why? D'you know him?

RALEIGH: Yes, rather! We were at school together—at least—of course—I was only a kid and he was one of the big fellows; he's three years older than I am.

There is a pause; OSBORNE *seems to be waiting for* RALEIGH *to go on, then suddenly he says:*

OSBORNE: He's up in the front line at present, looking after the relief. (*Another pause.*) He's a splendid chap.

RALEIGH: *Isn't* he? He was skipper of Rugger at Barford, and kept wicket for the eleven. A jolly good bat, too.

OSBORNE: Did you play Rugger—and cricket?

RALEIGH: Oh, yes. Of course, I wasn't in the same class as Dennis—I say, I suppose I ought to call him Captain Stanhope?

OSBORNE: Just " Stanhope."

RALEIGH: I see. Thanks.

OSBORNE: Did you get your colours?

RALEIGH: I did for Rugger. Not cricket.

OSBORNE: Rugger and cricket seem a long way from here.

RALEIGH (*laughing*): They do, rather.

OSBORNE: We play a bit of soccer when we're out of the line

RALEIGH: Good!

OSBORNE (*thoughtfully*): So you were at school with Stanhope. (*Pause.*) I wonder if he'll remember you? I expect you've grown in the last three years.

RALEIGH: Oh, I think he'll remember me. (*He stops, and goes on rather awkwardly.*) You see, it wasn't only that we were just at school together; our fathers were friends, and Dennis used to come and stay with us in the holidays. Of course, at school I didn't see much of him, but in the holidays we were terrific pals.

OSBORNE: He's a fine company commander.

RALEIGH: I bet he is. Last time he was on leave he came down to the school; he'd just got his M.C. and been made a captain. He looked splendid! It—sort of—made me feel——

OSBORNE: —keen?

RALEIGH: Yes. Keen to get out here. I was frightfully keen to get into Dennis's regiment. I thought, perhaps, with a bit of luck I might get to the same battalion.

OSBORNE: It's a big fluke to have got to the same company.

RALEIGH: I know. It's an amazing bit of luck. When I was at the base I did an awful thing. You see, my uncle's at the base—he has to detail officers to regiments——

OSBORNE: General Raleigh?

RALEIGH: Yes. I went to see him on the quiet and asked him if he could get me into this battalion. He bit my head off, and said I'd got to be treated like everybody else——

OSBORNE: Yes?

RALEIGH: —and next day I was told I *was* coming to this battalion. Funny, wasn't it?

OSBORNE: Extraordinary coincidence!

RALEIGH: And when I got to Battalion Headquarters, and the colonel told me to report to " C " Company, I could have cheered. I expect Dennis'll be frightfully surprised to see me. I've got a message for him.

OSBORNE: From the colonel?

RALEIGH: No. From my sister.

OSBORNE: Your sister?

RALEIGH: Yes. You see, Dennis used to stay with us, and naturally my sister (*he hesitates*)—well—perhaps I ought not——

OSBORNE: That's all right. I didn't actually know that Stanhope——

RALEIGH: They're not—er—officially engaged——

OSBORNE: No?

RALEIGH: She'll be awfully glad I'm with him here; I can write and tell her all about him. He doesn't say much in his letters; can we write often?

OSBORNE: Oh, yes. Letters are collected every day.

There is a pause.

RALEIGH: You don't think Dennis'll mind my—sort of—forcing myself into his company? I never thought of that; I was so keen.

OSBORNE: No, of course he won't. (*Pause.*) You say it's—it's a good time since you last saw him?

RALEIGH: Let's see. It was in the summer last year—nearly a year ago.

OSBORNE: You know, Raleigh, you mustn't expect to find him—quite the same.

RALEIGH: Oh?

OSBORNE: You see, he's been out here a long time. It—it tells on a man—rather badly——

RALEIGH (*thinking*): Yes, of course, I suppose it does.

OSBORNE: You may find he's—he's a little bit quick-tempered.

RALEIGH (*laughing*): Oh, I know old Dennis's temper! I remember once at school he caught some chaps in a study with a bottle of whisky. Lord! the roof nearly blew off. He gave them a dozen each with a cricket stump.

OSBORNE *laughs.*

He was so keen on the fellows in the house keeping fit. He was frightfully down on smoking—and that sort of thing.

OSBORNE: You must remember he's commanded this company for a long time—through all sorts of rotten times. It's—it's a big strain on a man.

RALEIGH: Oh, it must be.

OSBORNE: If you notice a—difference in Stanhope—you'll know it's only the strain——

RALEIGH: Oh, yes.

OSBORNE *rouses himself and speaks briskly.*

OSBORNE: Now, let's see. We've got five beds here—one each. Two in here and three in that dug-out there. I'm afraid you'll have to wait until the others come and pick the beds they want.

RALEIGH: Righto!

OSBORNE: Have you got a blanket.

RALEIGH: Yes, in my pack. (*He rises to get it.*)

OSBORNE: Better wait and unpack when you know where you are sleeping.

RALEIGH: Righto! (*He sits down again.*)

OSBORNE: We never undress when we're in the line. You can take your boots off now and then in the daytime, but it's better to keep pretty well dressed always.

RALEIGH: I see.   Thanks.

OSBORNE: I expect we shall each do about three hours on duty at a time and then six off. We all go on duty at stand-to. That's at dawn and dusk.

RALEIGH: Yes.

OSBORNE: I expect Stanhope'll send you on duty with one of us at first—till you get used to it.

There is a pause. RALEIGH *turns, and looks curiously up the steps into the night.*

RALEIGH: Are we in the front line here?

OSBORNE: No. That's the support line outside. The front line's about fifty yards farther on.

RALEIGH: How frightfully quiet it is!

OSBORNE: It's often quiet—like this.

RALEIGH: I thought there would be an awful row here—all the time.

OSBORNE: Most people think that.

Pause.

RALEIGH: I've never known anything so quiet as those trenches we came by; just now and then I heard rifle firing, like the range at Bisley,[1] and a sort of rumble in the distance.

[1] Bisley—famous shooting range.

OSBORNE: Those are the guns up north—up Wipers[1] way. The guns are always going up there; it's never quiet like this. (*Pause.*) I expect it's all very strange to you?

RALEIGH: It's—it's not exactly what I thought. It's just this—this quiet that seems so funny.

OSBORNE: A hundred yards from here the Germans are sitting in *their* dug-outs, thinking how quiet it is.

RALEIGH: Are they as near as that?

OSBORNE: About a hundred yards.

RALEIGH: It seems—uncanny. It makes me feel we're—we're all just waiting for something.

OSBORNE: We are, generally, just waiting for something. When anything happens, it happens quickly. Then we just start waiting again.

RALEIGH: I never thought it was like that.

OSBORNE: You thought it was fighting all the time?

RALEIGH (*laughing*): Well, yes, in a way.

OSBORNE (*after puffing at his pipe in silence for a while*): Did you come up by trench tonight—or over the top?

RALEIGH: By trench. An amazing trench—turning and twisting for miles, over a sort of plain.

OSBORNE: Lancer's Alley it's called.

RALEIGH: Is it? It's funny the way it begins—in that ruined village, a few steps down into the cellar of a house—then right under the house and through a little garden—and then under the garden wall—then alongside an enormous ruined factory place—then miles and miles of plains, with those green lights bobbing up and down ahead—all along the front as far as you can see.

OSBORNE: Those are the Very lights. Both sides fire them over No Man's Land—to watch for raids and patrols.

RALEIGH: I knew they fired lights. (*Pause.*) I didn't expect so many—and to see them so far away.

[1] Wipers—English soldiers' pronunciation of Ypres, where there was heavy fighting which destroyed the town.

OSBORNE: I know. (*He puffs at his pipe.*) There's something rather romantic about it all.

RALEIGH (*eagerly*): Yes. I thought that, too.

OSBORNE: You must always think of it like that if you can. Think of it all as—as romantic. It helps.

MASON *comes in with more dinner utensils.*

MASON: D'you expect the captain soon, sir? The soup's 'ot.

OSBORNE: He ought to be here very soon now. This is Mr. Raleigh, Mason.

MASON: Good evening, sir.

RALEIGH: Good evening.

MASON (*to* OSBORNE): I've 'ad rather a unpleasant surprise, sir.

OSBORNE: What's happened?

MASON: You know that tin o' pineapple chunks I got, sir?

OSBORNE: Yes?

MASON: Well, sir, I'm sorry to say it's apricots.

OSBORNE: Good heavens! It must have given you a turn.

MASON: I distinctly said " Pineapple chunks " at the canteen.

OSBORNE: Wasn't there a label on the tin?

MASON: No, sir. I pointed that out to the man. I said was 'e *certain* it was pineapple chunks?

OSBORNE: I suppose he said he was.

MASON: Yes, sir. 'E said a leopard can't change its spots, sir.

OSBORNE: What have leopards got to do with pineapple?

MASON: That's just what *I* thought, sir. Made me *think* there was something fishy about it. You see, sir, I know the captain can't stand the sight of apricots. 'E said next time we 'ad them 'e'd wring my neck.

OSBORNE: Haven't you anything else?

MASON: There's a pink blancmange I've made, sir. But it ain't anywhere near stiff yet.

OSBORNE: Never mind. We must have the apricots and chance it.

MASON: Only I thought I'd tell you, sir, so as the captain wouldn't blame me.

OSBORNE: All right, Mason.

Voices are heard in the trench above.

That sounds like the captain coming now.

MASON (*hastening away*): I'll go and dish out the soup, sir.

The voices grow nearer; two figures appear in the trench above and grope down the steps—the leading figure tall and slim, the other short and fat. The tall figure is CAPTAIN STANHOPE. *At the bottom of the steps he straightens himself, pulls off his pack, and drops it on the floor. Then he takes off his helmet and throws it on the right-hand bed. Despite his stars of rank he is no more than a boy; tall, slimly built, but broad-shouldered. His dark hair is carefully brushed; his uniform, though old and war-stained, is well cut and cared for. He is good-looking, rather from attractive features than the healthy good looks of* RALEIGH. *Although tanned by months in the open air, there is a pallor under his skin and dark shadows under his eyes. His short and fat companion—2ND LIEUTENANT TROTTER—is middle-aged and homely looking. His face is red, fat, and round; apparently he has put on weight during his war service, for his tunic appears to be on the verge of bursting at the waist. He carries an extra pack belonging to the officer left on duty in the line.*

STANHOPE (*as he takes off his pack, gas satchel, and belt*): Has Hardy gone?

OSBORNE: Yes. He cleared off a few minutes ago.

STANHOPE: Lucky for him he did. I had a few words to say to Master Hardy. You never saw the blasted mess those fellows left the trenches in. Dug-outs smell like cess-pits; rusty bombs; damp rifle grenades; it's perfectly foul. Where are the servants?

OSBORNE: In there.

STANHOPE (*calling into* MASON's *dug-out*): Hi! Mason!

MASON (*outside*): Coming, sir! Just bringing the soup, sir.

STANHOPE (*taking a cigarette from his case and lighting it*): Damn the soup! Bring some whisky!

OSBORNE: Here's a new officer, Stanhope—just arrived.

STANHOPE: Oh, sorry. (*He turns and peers into the dim corner where* RALEIGH *stands smiling awkwardly.*) I didn't see you in this miserable light. (*He stops short at the sight of* RALEIGH. *There is silence.*)

RALEIGH: Hullo, Stanhope!

STANHOPE *stares at* RALEIGH *as though dazed.* RALEIGH *takes a step forward, half raises his hand, then lets it drop to his side.*

STANHOPE (*in a low voice*): How did you—get here?

RALEIGH: I was told to report to your company, Stanhope.

STANHOPE: Oh. I see. Rather a coincidence.

RALEIGH (*with a nervous laugh*): Yes.

There is a silence for a moment, broken by OSBORNE *in a matter-of-fact voice.*

OSBORNE: I say, Stanhope, it's a terrible business. We thought we'd got a tin of pineapple chunks; it turns out to be apricots.

TROTTER: Ha! Give me apricots every time! I 'ate pineapple chunks; too bloomin' sickly for me!

RALEIGH: I'm awfully glad I got to your company, Stanhope.

STANHOPE: When did you get here?

RALEIGH: Well, I've only just come.

OSBORNE: He came up with the transport while you were taking over.

STANHOPE: I see.

MASON *brings in a bottle of whisky, a mug, and two plates of soup—so precariously that* OSBORNE *has to help with the soup plates on to the table.*

STANHOPE (*with sudden forced gaiety*): Come along, Uncle! Come and sit here. (*He waves towards the box on the right of the table.*) You better sit there, Raleigh.

RALEIGH: Right!

TROTTER (*taking a pair of pince-nez from his tunic pocket, putting them on, and looking curiously at* RALEIGH): You Raleigh?

RALEIGH: Yes.

Pause.

TROTTER: I'm Trotter.

RALEIGH: Oh, yes?

Pause.

TROTTER: How *are* you?

RALEIGH: Oh, all right, thanks.

TROTTER: Been out 'ere before?

RALEIGH: No.

TROTTER: Feel a bit odd, I s'pose?

RALEIGH: Yes.   A bit.

TROTTER (*getting a box to sit on*): Oh, well, you'll soon get used to it; you'll feel you've been 'ere a year in about an hour's time. (*He puts the box on its side and sits on it. It is too low for the table, and he puts it on its end. It is then too high. He tries the other side, which is too low; he finally contrives to make himself comfortable by sitting on his pack, placed on the side of the box.*)

MASON *arrives with two more plates of soup.*

OSBORNE: What kind of soup is this, Mason?

MASON: It's yellow soup, sir.

OSBORNE: It's got a very deep yellow flavour.

TROTTER (*taking a melodious sip*): It wants some pepper; bring some pepper, Mason.

MASON (*anxiously*): I'm very sorry, sir. When the mess box was packed the pepper was omitted, sir.

TROTTER (*throwing his spoon with a clatter into the plate*): Oh, I say, but damn it!

OSBORNE: We must have pepper. It's a disinfectant.

TROTTER: You must have pepper in soup!

STANHOPE (*quietly*): Why wasn't it packed, Mason?

MASON: It—it was missed, sir.

STANHOPE: Why?

MASON (*miserably*): Well, sir, I left it to——

STANHOPE: Then I advise you never to leave it to anyone else again—unless you want to rejoin your platoon out there. (*He points into the moonlit trench.*)

MASON: I'm—I'm very sorry, sir.

STANHOPE: Send one of the signallers.

MASON: Yes, sir.

He hastens to the tunnel entrance and calls:
Bert, you're wanted!

A SOLDIER appears, with a rifle slung over his shoulder. He stands stiffly to attention.

STANHOPE: Do you know " A " Company Headquarters?

SOLDIER: Yes, sir.

STANHOPE: Go there at once and ask Captain Willis, with my compliments, if he can lend me a little pepper.

SOLDIER: Very good, sir.

He turns smartly and goes up the steps, MASON stopping him for a moment to say confidentially:
" A *screw* of pepper, you ask for."

OSBORNE: We must have pepper.

TROTTER: I mean—after all—war's bad enough *with* pepper— (*noisy sip*)—but war without pepper—it's—it's bloody awful!

OSBORNE: What's it like outside?

TROTTER: Quiet as an empty 'ouse. There's a nasty noise going on up north.

OSBORNE: Wipers, I expect. I believe there's trouble up there. I wish we knew more of what's going on.

TROTTER: So do I. Still, my wife reads the papers every morning and writes and tells me.

OSBORNE: Hardy says they had a lively time here yesterday. Three big Minnies right in the trench.

TROTTER: I know. And they left the bloomin' 'oles for us to fill in.

MASON arrives with cutlets on enamel plates.

What's this.

MASON: Meat, sir.

TROTTER: I know that.   What sort?

MASON: Sort of cutlet, sir.

TROTTER: Sort of cutlet, is it? You know, Mason, there's cutlets and cutlets.

MASON: I know, sir; that one's a cutlet.

TROTTER: Well, it won't let me cut it.

MASON: No, sir?

TROTTER: That's a joke.

MASON: Oh.   Right, sir.

He goes out.

OSBORNE (*studying the map*): There's a sort of ruin marked on this map—just in front of here, in No Man's Land—called Beauvais Farm.

TROTTER: That's what we saw sticking up, skipper. I wondered what it was.

STANHOPE: Better go out and look at it tonight.

TROTTER: I expect a nasty German'll 'op out of it and say, " Ock der Kaiser."[1] I 'ate ruins in No Man's Land.

OSBORNE: There's only about sixty yards of No Man's Land, according to this map—narrower on the left, from the head of this sap; only about fifty.

TROTTER (*who has been looking curiously at* STANHOPE, *eating his meal with lowered head*): Cheer up, skipper. You *do* look glum!

STANHOPE: I'm tired.

OSBORNE: I should turn in and get some sleep after supper.

STANHOPE: I've got hours of work before I sleep.

OSBORNE: I'll do the duty roll and see the sergeant-major—and all that.

STANHOPE: That's all right, Uncle. I'll see to it. (*He turns to* RALEIGH *for the first time.*) Trotter goes on duty directly he's had supper. You better go on with him—to learn.

RALEIGH: Oh, right.

TROTTER: Look 'ere, skipper, it's nearly eight now; couldn't we make it 'alf-past?

[1] Ock der Kaiser—in German " Hoch der Kaiser " or " Up with the Kaiser." The Kaiser was the last German emperor.

STANHOPE: No. I told Hibbert he'd be relieved at eight. Will you take from eleven till two, Uncle?

OSBORNE: Right.

STANHOPE: Hibbert can do from two till four, and I'll go on from then till stand-to. That'll be at six.

TROTTER: Well, boys! 'Ere we are for six days again. Six bloomin' eternal days. (*He makes a calculation on the table.*) That's a hundred and forty-four hours; eight thousand six 'undred and forty minutes. *That* doesn't sound so bad; we've done twenty of 'em already. I've got an idea! I'm going to draw a hundred and forty-four little circles on a bit o' paper, and every hour I'm going to black one in; that'll make the time go all right.

STANHOPE: It's five to eight now. You better go and relieve Hibbert. Then you can come back at eleven o'clock and black in three of your bloody little circles.

TROTTER: I 'aven't 'ad my apricots yet!

STANHOPE: We'll keep your apricots till you come back.

TROTTER: I never knew anything like a war for upsetting meals. I'm always down for dooty in the middle of one.

STANHOPE: That's because you never stop eating.

TROTTER: Any'ow, let's 'ave some coffee. Hi! Mason! Coffee!

MASON: Coming, sir!

TROTTER (*getting up*): Well, I'll get dressed. Come on, Raleigh.

RALEIGH (*rising quickly*): Right!

TROTTER: Just wear your belt with revolver case on it. Must have your revolver to shoot rats. And your gas mask—come here—I'll show you. (*He helps* RALEIGH.) You wear it sort of tucked up under your chin like a serviette.

RALEIGH: Yes. I was shown the way at home.

TROTTER: Now your hat. That's right. You don't want a walking-stick. It gets in your way if you have to run fast.

RALEIGH: Why—er—do you have to run fast?

TROTTER: Oh, Lord, yes, often! If you see a Minnie coming— that's a big trench-mortar shell, you know—short for *Minnywerfer*—you see 'em come right out of the Boche trenches, right up in the air, then down, down, down; and you have to judge it and run like stink sometimes.

MASON *comes in with two cups of coffee.*

MASON: Coffee, sir?

TROTTER: Thanks. (*He takes the cup and drinks standing up.*)

RALEIGH: Thanks.

TROTTER: You might leave my apricots out, Mason. Put 'em on a separate plate and keep 'em in there. (*He points to* MASON's *dug-out.*)

MASON: Very good, sir.

TROTTER: If you bring 'em in 'ere you never know *what* might 'appen to 'em.

MASON: No, sir.

TROTTER: " B " Company on our right, aren't they, skipper?

STANHOPE: Yes. There's fifty yards of undefended area between. You better patrol that a good deal.

TROTTER: Aye, aye, sir.

STANHOPE: Have a look at that Lewis gun position on the left. See what field of fire they've got.

TROTTER: Aye, aye, sir. You don't want me to go out and look at that blinkin' ruin?

STANHOPE: I'll see to that.

TROTTER: Good. I don't fancy crawling about on my belly after that cutlet. (*To* RALEIGH) Well, come on, my lad, let's go and see about this 'ere war.

The two go up the steps, leaving STANHOPE *and* OSBORNE *alone.*

MASON *appears at his dug-out door.*

MASON: Will you take apricots, sir?

STANHOPE: No, thanks.

MASON: Mr. Osborne?

OSBORNE: No, thanks.

MASON: I'm sorry about them being apricots, sir. I explained to Mr. Osborne——

STANHOPE (*curtly*): That's all right, Mason—thank you.

MASON: Very good, sir.

He goes out.

OSBORNE (*over by the right-hand bed*): Will you sleep here? This was Hardy's bed.

STANHOPE: No. You sleep there. I'd rather sleep by the table here. I can get up and work without disturbing you.

OSBORNE: This is a better one.

STANHOPE: You take it. Must have a little comfort in your old age, Uncle.

OSBORNE: I wish you'd turn in and sleep for a bit.

STANHOPE: Sleep?—I can't sleep. (*He takes a whisky and water.*) *A man appears in the trench and comes down the steps—a small, slightly built man in the early twenties, with a little moustache and a pallid face.*

(*Looking hard at the newcomer.*) Well, Hibbert?

HIBBERT: Everything's fairly quiet. Bit of sniping somewhere to our left; some rifle grenades coming over just on our right.

STANHOPE: I see.   Mason's got your supper.

HIBBERT (*gently rubbing his forehead*): I don't think I can manage any supper tonight, Stanhope. It's this beastly neuralgia. It seems to be right inside this eye. The beastly pain gets worse every day.

STANHOPE: Some hot soup and a good tough chop'll put that right.

HIBBERT: I'm afraid the pain rather takes my appetite away. I'm damn sorry to keep on talking about it, Stanhope, only I thought you'd wonder why I don't eat anything much.

STANHOPE: Try and forget about it.

HIBBERT (*with a little laugh*): Well—I wish I could.

STANHOPE: Get tight.

HIBBERT: I think I'll turn straight in for a rest—and try and get some sleep.

STANHOPE: All right. Turn in. You're in that dug-out there. Here's your pack. (*He picks up the pack that* TROTTER *brought down.*) You go on duty at two. I take over from you at four. I'll tell Mason to call you.

HIBBERT (*faintly*): Oh, right—thanks, Stanhope—cheero.

STANHOPE: Cheero. (*He watches* HIBBERT *go down the tunnel into the dark.*)

HIBBERT (*returning*): Can I have a candle?

STANHOPE (*taking one from the table*): Here you are.

HIBBERT: Thanks.

He goes out again. There is silence. STANHOPE *turns to* OSBORNE.

STANHOPE: Another little worm trying to wriggle home.

OSBORNE (*filling his pipe*): I wonder if he really is bad. He looks rotten.

STANHOPE: Pure bloody funk, that's all. He could eat if he wanted to; he's starving himself purposely. Artful little swine! Neuralgia's a splendid idea. No proof, as far as I can see.

OSBORNE: You can't help feeling sorry for him. I think he's tried hard.

STANHOPE: How long's he been out here? Three months, I suppose. Now he's decided he's done his bit. He's decided to go home and spend the rest of the war in comfortable nerve hospitals. Well, he's mistaken. I let Warren get away like that, but no more.

OSBORNE: I don't see how you can prevent a fellow going sick.

STANHOPE: I'll have a quiet word with the doctor before *he* does. He thinks he's going to wriggle off before the attack. We'll just see about that. No man of mine's going sick before the attack. They're going to take an equal chance—together.

OSBORNE: Raleigh looks a nice chap.

STANHOPE (*looking hard at* OSBORNE *before replying*): Yes.

OSBORNE: Good-looking youngster. At school with you, wasn't he?

STANHOPE: Has he been talking already?

OSBORNE: He just mentioned it. It was a natural thing to tell me when he knew you were in command.

STANHOPE *is lounging at the table with his back to the wall.* OSBORNE, *sitting on the right-hand bed, begins to puff clouds of smoke into the air as he lights his pipe.*

He's awfully pleased to get into your company.

STANHOPE *makes no reply. He picks up a pencil and scribbles on the back of a magazine.*

He seems to think a lot of you.

STANHOPE (*looking up quickly at* OSBORNE *and laughing*): Yes, I'm his hero.

OSBORNE: It's quite natural.

STANHOPE: You think so?

OSBORNE: Small boys at school generally have their heroes.

STANHOPE: Yes.   Small boys at school do.

OSBORNE: Often it goes on as long as——

STANHOPE: —as long as the hero's a hero.

OSBORNE: It often goes on all through life.

STANHOPE: I wonder. How many battalions are there in France?

OSBORNE: Why?

STANHOPE: We'll say fifty divisions. That's a hundred and fifty brigades—four hundred and fifty battalions. That's one thousand eight hundred companies. (*He looks up at* OSBORNE *from his calculations on the magazine cover.*) There are one thousand eight hundred companies in France, Uncle. Raleigh might have been sent to any one of those, and, my God! he comes to mine.

OSBORNE: You ought to be glad. He's a good-looking youngster. I like him.

STANHOPE: I knew you'd like him. Personality, isn't it? (*He takes a worn leather case from his breast pocket and hands a small photograph to* OSBORNE.) I've never shown you that, have I?

OSBORNE (*looking at the photograph*): No. (*Pause.*) Raleigh's sister, isn't it?

STANHOPE: How did you know?

OSBORNE: There's a strong likeness.

STANHOPE: I suppose there is.

OSBORNE (*intent on the picture*): She's an awfully nice-looking girl.

STANHOPE: A photo doesn't show much, really. Just a face.

Osborne: She looks awfully nice.

There is silence. Stanhope *lights a cigarette.* Osborne *hands the photo back.*

You're a lucky chap.

Stanhope (*putting the photo back into his case*): I don't know why I keep it, really.

Osborne: Why? Isn't she—I thought——

Stanhope: What did you think?

Osborne: Well, I thought that perhaps she was waiting for you.

Stanhope: Yes. She is waiting for me—and she doesn't know. She thinks I'm a wonderful chap—commanding a company. (*He turns to* Osborne *and points up the steps into the line.*) She doesn't know that if I went up those steps into the front line—without being doped with whisky—I'd go mad with fright.

There is a pause. Osborne *stirs himself to speak.*

Osborne: Look here, old man. I've meant to say it, for a long time, but it sounds damned impudence. You've done longer out here than any man in the battalion. It's time you went away for a rest. It's due to you.

Stanhope: You suggest that I go sick, like that little worm in there—neuralgia in the eye? (*He laughs and takes a drink.*)

Osborne: No. Not that. The colonel would have sent you down long ago, only——

Stanhope: Only—what?

Osborne: Only he can't spare you.

Stanhope (*laughing*): Oh, rot!

Osborne: He told me.

Stanhope: He thinks I'm in such a state I want a rest, is that it?

Osborne: No. He thinks it's due to you.

Stanhope: It's all right, Uncle. I'll stick it out now. It may not be much longer now. I've had my share of luck—more than my share. There's not a man left who was here when I came. But it's rather damnable for that boy—of all the boys in the world—to have come to *me*. I might at least have been spared that.

OSBORNE: You're looking at things in rather a black sort of way.

STANHOPE: I've just told you. That boy's a hero-worshipper. I'm three years older than he is. You know what that means at school. I was skipper of Rugger and all that sort of thing. It doesn't sound much to a man out here—but it does at school with a kid of fourteen. Damn it, Uncle, you're a schoolmaster; you know.

OSBORNE: I've just told you what I think of hero-worship.

STANHOPE: Raleigh's father knew mine, and I was told to keep an eye on the kid. I rather liked the idea of looking after him. I made him keen on the right things—and all that. His people asked me to stay with them one summer. I met his sister then——

OSBORNE: Yes?

STANHOPE: At first I thought of her as another kid like Raleigh. It was just before I came out here for the first time that I realised what a topping girl she was. Funny how you realise it suddenly. I just prayed to come through the war—and—and *do* things—and keep absolutely fit for her.

OSBORNE: You've done pretty well. An M.C. and a company.

STANHOPE (*taking another whisky*): It was all right at first. When I went home on leave after six months it was jolly fine to feel I'd done a little to make her pleased. (*He takes a gulp of his drink.*) It was after I came back here—in that awful affair on Vimy Ridge.[1] I knew I'd go mad if I didn't break the strain. I couldn't bear being fully conscious all the time—*you've* felt that, Uncle, haven't you?

OSBORNE: Yes, often.

STANHOPE: There were only two ways of breaking the strain. One was pretending I was ill—and going home; the other was this. (*He holds up his glass.*) Which would you pick, Uncle?

OSBORNE: I haven't been through as much as you. I don't know yet.

STANHOPE: I thought it all out. It's a slimy thing to go home if you're not really ill, isn't it?

OSBORNE: I think it is.

[1] Vimy Ridge—one of the points on the front where there was terrible loss of life.

STANHOPE: Well, then. (*He holds his glass up to* OSBORNE.) Cheero, and long live the men who go home with neuralgia. (*He puts his glass down.*) I didn't go home on my last leave. I couldn't bear to meet her, in case she realised——

OSBORNE: When the war's over—and the strain's gone—you'll soon be as fit as ever, at your age.

STANHOPE: I've hoped that all the time. I'd go away for months and live in the open air—and get fit—and then go back to her.

OSBORNE: And so you can.

STANHOPE: If Raleigh had gone to one of those other one thousand eight hundred companies.

OSBORNE: I don't see why you should think——

STANHOPE: Oh, for Lord's sake don't be a damn fool. *You* know! You know he'll write and tell her I reek of whisky all day.

OSBORNE: Why should he? He's not a——

STANHOPE: Exactly. He's not a damned little swine who'd deceive his sister.

OSBORNE: He's very young; he's got hundreds of strange things to learn; he'll realise that men are—*different*—out here.

STANHOPE: It's no good, Uncle. Didn't you see him sitting there at supper?—staring at me?—and wondering? He's up in those trenches now—still wondering—and beginning to understand. And all these months he's wanted to be with me out here. Poor little devil!

OSBORNE: I believe Raleigh'll go on liking you—and looking up to you—through everything. There's something very deep, and rather fine, about hero-worship.

STANHOPE: Hero-worship be damned! (*He pauses, then goes on, in a strange, high-pitched voice.*) You know, Uncle, I'm an *awful* fool. I'm *captain* of this company. What's that bloody little prig of a boy matter? D'you see? He's a little prig. Wants to write home and tell Madge all about *me*. Well, he won't; d'you see, Uncle? He *won't* write. Censorship! I censor his letters—cross out all he says about me.

OSBORNE: You can't read his letters.

STANHOPE (*dreamily*): Cross out all he says about me. Then we all go west in the big attack—and she goes on thinking I'm a fine fellow for ever—and ever—and ever. (*He pours out a drink, murmuring* " *Ever—and ever—and ever.*")

OSBORNE (*rising from his bed*): It's not as bad as all that. Turn in and have a sleep.

STANHOPE: Sleep! Catch *me* wasting my time with sleep.

OSBORNE (*picking up* STANHOPE'S *pack and pulling out the blanket*): Come along, old chap. You come and lie down here. (*He puts the pack as a pillow on* STANHOPE'S *bed, and spreads out the blanket.*)

STANHOPE (*with his chin in his hands*): Little prig—that's what he is. Did *I* ask him to force his way into my company? No! I didn't. Very well, he'll pay for his damn cheek.

OSBORNE *lays his hand gently on* STANHOPE'S *shoulder to persuade him to lie down.*
Go away! (*He shakes* OSBORNE'S *hand off.*) What the hell are you trying to do?

OSBORNE: Come and lie down and go to sleep.

STANHOPE: Go sleep y'self. I censor his letters, d'you see, Uncle? You watch and see he doesn't smuggle any letters away.

OSBORNE: Righto. Now come and lie down. You've had a hard day of it.

STANHOPE (*looking up suddenly*): Where's Hardy? D'you say he's gone?

OSBORNE: Yes. He's gone.

STANHOPE: Gone, has he? Y'know, I had a word to say to Master Hardy. He would go, the swine! Dirty trenches— everything dirty—I wanner tell him to keep his trenches clean.

OSBORNE (*standing beside* STANHOPE *and putting his hand gently on his shoulder again*): We'll clean them up to-morrow.

STANHOPE *looks up at* OSBORNE *and laughs gaily.*

STANHOPE: Dear old Uncle! Clean trenches up—with little dustpan and brush. (*He laughs.*) Make you little apron—with lace on it.

OSBORNE: That'll be fine. Now then, come along, old chap. I'll see you get called at two o'clock. (*He firmly takes* STANHOPE *by the arm and draws him over to the bed.*) You *must* be tired.

STANHOPE (*in a dull voice*): God, I'm bloody tired; ache—all over—feel sick.

OSBORNE *helps him on to the bed, takes the blanket and puts it over him.*

OSBORNE: You'll feel all right in a minute. How's that? Comfortable?

STANHOPE: Yes. Comfortable. (*He looks up into* OSBORNE'S *face and laughs again.*) Dear old Uncle. Tuck me up.

OSBORNE *fumbles the blankets round* STANHOPE.

OSBORNE: There we are.

STANHOPE: Kiss me, Uncle.

OSBORNE: Kiss you be blowed! You go to sleep.

STANHOPE (*closing his eyes*): Yes—I go sleep. (*He turns slowly on to his side with his face to the earth wall.*)

OSBORNE *stands watching for a while, then blows out the candle by* STANHOPE'S *bed.* STANHOPE *gives a deep sigh, and begins to breathe heavily.* OSBORNE *goes to the servant's dug-out and calls softly:*

OSBORNE: Mason!

MASON (*appearing with unbuttoned tunic at the tunnel entrance*): Yessir?

OSBORNE: Will you call me at ten minutes to eleven—and Mr. Hibbert at ten minutes to two? I'm going to turn in for a little while.

MASON: Very good, sir. (*Pause.*) The pepper's come, sir.

OSBORNE: Oh, good.

MASON: I'm very sorry about the pepper, sir.

OSBORNE: That's all right, Mason.

MASON: Good night, sir.

OSBORNE: Good night.

MASON *leaves the dug-out.* OSBORNE *turns, and looks up the narrow steps into the night, where the Very lights rise and fade against the starlit sky. He glances once more at* STANHOPE, *then crosses to his own bed, takes out from his tunic pocket a large, old-fashioned watch, and quietly winds it up.*

Through the stillness comes the low rumble of distant guns.

THE CURTAIN FALLS

ACT II

Early next morning.

A pale shaft of sunlight shines down the steps, but candles still burn in the dark corner where OSBORNE *and* RALEIGH *are at breakfast.* MASON *has put a large plate of bacon before each, and turns to go as* TROTTER *comes down the steps, whistling gaily and rubbing his hands.*

TROTTER: What a lovely smell of bacon!

MASON: Yes, sir. I reckon there's enough smell of bacon in 'ere to last for dinner.

TROTTER: Well, there's nothing like a good fat bacon rasher when you're as empty as I am.

MASON: I'm glad you like it fat, sir.

TROTTER: Well, I like a bit o' lean, too.

MASON: There *was* a bit of lean in the middle of yours, sir, but it's kind of shrunk up in the cooking.

TROTTER: Bad cooking, that's all. Any porridge?

MASON: Oh, yes, sir. There's porridge.

TROTTER: Lumpy, I s'pose?

MASON: Yes. sir. Quite nice and lumpy.

TROTTER: Well, take the lumps out o' mine.

MASON: And just bring you the gravy, sir? Very good, sir.

MASON *goes out.* TROTTER *looks after him suspiciously.*

TROTTER: You know, that man's getting familiar.

OSBORNE: He's not a bad cook.

TROTTER *has picked up his coffee mug, and is smelling it.*

TROTTER: I say, d'you realise he's washed his dish-cloth?

OSBORNE: I know. I told him about it.

TROTTER: Did you really? You've got some pluck. 'Ow did you go about it?

OSBORNE: I wrote and asked my wife for a packet of Lux. Then I gave it to Mason and suggested he tried it on something.

TROTTER: Good man. No, he's not a bad cook. Might be a lot worse. When I was in the ranks we 'ad a prize cook—used to be a plumber before the war. Ought to 'ave seen the stew 'e made. Thin! Thin wasn't the word. Put a bucketful of 'is stew in a bath and pull the plug, and the whole lot would go down in a couple of gurgles.

MASON *brings* TROTTER'S *porridge*.

MASON: I've took the lumps out.

TROTTER: Good. Keep 'em and use 'em for dumplings next time we 'ave boiled beef.

MASON: Very good, sir.

He goes out.

TROTTER: Yes. That plumber was a prize cook, 'e was. Lucky for us one day 'e set 'imself on fire making the tea. 'E went 'ome pretty well fried. Did Mason get that pepper?

OSBORNE: Yes.

TROTTER: Good. Must 'ave pepper.

OSBORNE: I thought you were on duty now.

TROTTER: I'm supposed to be. Stanhope sent me down to get my breakfast. He's looking after things till I finish.

OSBORNE: He's got a long job then.

TROTTER: Oh, no. I'm a quick eater. Hi! Mason! Bacon!

MASON (*outside*): Coming, sir!

OSBORNE: It's a wonderful morning.

TROTTER: Isn't it lovely? Makes you feel sort of young and 'opeful. I was up in that old trench under the brick wall just now, and damned if a bloomin' little bird didn't start singing! Didn't 'arf sound funny. Sign of spring, I s'pose.

MASON *arrives with* TROTTER'S *bacon*.

That looks all right.

MASON: If you look down straight on it from above, sir, you can see the bit o' lean quite clear.

TROTTER: Good Lord, yes! That's it, isn't it?

MASON: No, sir; that's a bit o' rust off the pan.

TROTTER: Ah! *That's* it, then!

MASON: You've got it, sir.

He goes out.

TROTTER: Cut us a chunk of bread, Uncle.

OSBORNE *cuts him off a chunk.*

OSBORNE: How are things going up there?

TROTTER: I don't like the look of things a bit.

OSBORNE: You mean—the quiet?

TROTTER: Yes. Standing up there in the dark last night there didn't seem a thing in the world alive—except the rats squeaking and my stomach grumbling about the cutlet.

OSBORNE: It's quiet even now.

TROTTER: Too damn quiet. You can bet your boots the Boche is up to something. The big attack soon, I reckon. I don't like it, Uncle. Pass the jam.

OSBORNE: It's strawberry.

TROTTER: Is it? I'm glad we've got rid o' that raspberry jam. Can't stand raspberry jam. Pips get be'ind your plate.

OSBORNE: Did Stanhope tell you he wants two wiring parties out tonight?

TROTTER: Yes. He's fixing it up now. (*He pauses, and goes on in a low voice.*) My goodness, Uncle, doesn't he look ill!

OSBORNE: I'm afraid he's not well.

TROTTER: Nobody'd be well who went on like he does. (*There is another pause.*) You know when you came up to relieve me last night?

OSBORNE: Yes?

TROTTER: Well, Raleigh and me came back here, and there was Stanhope sitting on that bed drinking a whisky. He looked as white as a sheet. God, he looked awful; he'd drunk the bottle since dinner. I said, " 'Ullo! " and he didn't seem to know who I was. Uncanny, wasn't it, Raleigh?

RALEIGH (*with lowered head*): Yes.

TROTTER: He just said, " Better go to bed, Raleigh "—just as if Raleigh'd been a school kid.

OSBORNE: Did he? (*There is a pause.*) Look at the sun. It'll be quite warm soon.

They look at the pale square of sunlight on the floor.

TROTTER: It's warm now. You can feel it on your face outside if you stand in it. First time this year. 'Ope we 'ave an 'ot summer.

OSBORNE: So do I.

TROTTER: Funny about that bird. Made me feel quite braced up. Sort of made me think about my garden of an evening— walking round in me slippers after supper, smoking me pipe.

OSBORNE: You keen on gardening?

TROTTER: Oh, I used to do a bit of an evening. I 'ad a decent little grass plot in front, with flower-borders—geraniums, lobelia, and calceolaria—you know, red, white, and blue. Looked rather nice in the summer.

OSBORNE: Yes.

TROTTER: 'Ad some fine 'olly'ocks out the back. One year I 'ad one eight feet 'igh. Took a photer of it. (*He fumbles in his pocket case.*) Like to look at it?

OSBORNE: I would. (*He looks at the photo.*) By Jove, it's a beauty.

TROTTER (*looking over* OSBORNE's *shoulder*): You see that, just there?

OSBORNE: Yes?

TROTTER: That's the roof of the summer-'ouse.

OSBORNE: Is it really!

TROTTER: Just shows the 'ite of the 'olly'ock.

OSBORNE: It does. (*He shows the photo to* RALEIGH.) A beauty, isn't it?

RALEIGH: Rather!

TROTTER: It never wanted no stick to keep it straight, neether. (*There is a pause.*) You keen on gardening?

OSBORNE: Yes. A bit. I made a rockery when I was home on leave. I used to cycle out to the woods and get primroses and things like that, and try and get 'em to grow in my garden.

TROTTER: I don't suppose they would!

OSBORNE: They would if you pressed a bit of moss round them——

TROTTER: —to make 'em feel at 'ome, eh? (*He laughs.*)

OSBORNE: They'll be coming out again soon if they've got this sun at home.

TROTTER: I reckon they will. I remember one morning last spring—we was coming out of the salient.[1] Just when it was getting light in the morning—it was at the time when the Boche was sending over a lot of that gas that smells like pear-drops, you know?

OSBORNE: I know.   Phosgene.

TROTTER: That's it. We were scared to hell of it. All of a sudden we smelt that funny sweet smell, and a fellow shouted " Gas! "—and we put on our masks; and then I spotted what it was.

OSBORNE What was it?

TROTTER: Why, a blinkin' may-tree! All out in bloom, growing beside the path! We did feel a lot of silly poops—putting on gas masks because of a damn may-tree! (*He stretches himself and tries to button his tunic.*) Lord! I *must* get my fat down. (*He gets up.*) Well, I better go and relieve Stanhope. He'll curse like hell if I don't. I bet he's got a red-hot liver this morning.

OSBORNE: I relieve you at eleven.

TROTTER: That's right. I don't like this time of day in the line. The old Boche 'as just 'ad 'is breakfast, and sends over a few whizz-bangs and rifle grenades to show 'e ain't forgotten us. Still, I'd rather 'ave a bang or two than this damn quiet. (*He puts on his helmet and gas mask satchel and goes up the steps.*) Cheero!

OSBORNE: Cheero!

[1] Salient—a bulge in the line, where one side pushes forward in the hope of breaking through. The other side tries to " nip off " the salient and surround the troops occupying it. Heavy fighting results.

RALEIGH: Cheero!

OSBORNE (*to* RALEIGH): I expect Stanhope'll let you go on duty alone now.

RALEIGH: Will he?   About what time?

OSBORNE: Well, after me, I expect. From about two till four.

RALEIGH: I see.

There is a pause. Then OSBORNE *looks at* RALEIGH *and laughs.*

OSBORNE: What do you think about it all?

RALEIGH: Oh, all right, thanks. (*He laughs.*) I feel I've been here ages.

OSBORNE (*filling his pipe*): I expect you do. The time passes, though.

RALEIGH: Are we here for six days?

OSBORNE: Yes. Seems a long time, doesn't it?

RALEIGH (*laughing shortly*): It does rather. I can't imagine—the end of six days here——

OSBORNE: Anyhow, we've done twelve hours already. It's fine when you are relieved and go down the line to billets, and have a good hot bath, and sit and read under trees.

RALEIGH: Good Lord, I feel I haven't seen a tree for ages—not a real tree, with leaves and branches—and yet I've only been here twelve hours.

OSBORNE: How did you feel—in the front line?

RALEIGH: Oh, all right. It seemed so frightfully quiet and uncanny—everybody creeping about and talking in low voices. I suppose you've *got* to talk quietly when you're so near the German front line—only about seventy yards, isn't it?

OSBORNE: Yes. About the breadth of a Rugger field.

RALEIGH: It's funny to think of it like that.

OSBORNE: I always measure distances like that out here. Keeps them in proportion.

RALEIGH: Did you play Rugger?

OSBORNE: Yes. But mostly reffing at school in the last few years.

RALEIGH: Are you a schoolmaster, then?

OSBORNE: Yes. I must apologise.

RALEIGH: Oh, I don't mind schoolmasters. (*Hastily.*) I—I—mean, I never met one outside a school.

OSBORNE: They do get out sometimes.

RALEIGH (*laughing*): Who did you play for?

OSBORNE: The Harlequins.

RALEIGH: I say, really!

OSBORNE: I played for the English team on one great occasion.

RALEIGH: What! For *England*!

OSBORNE: I was awfully lucky to get the chance. It's a long time ago now.

RALEIGH (*with awe*): Oh, but, good Lord! that must have been simply topping. Where did you play?

OSBORNE: Wing three.

RALEIGH: I say, I—I never realised—you'd played for England?

OSBORNE: Tuppence to talk to me now! Anyhow, don't breeze it about.

RALEIGH: Don't the others know?

OSBORNE: We never talk about Rugger.

RALEIGH: They ought to know. It'd make them feel jolly bucked.

OSBORNE (*laughing*): It doesn't make much difference out here!

RALEIGH: It must be awfully thrilling, playing in front of a huge crowd—all shouting and cheering——

OSBORNE: You don't notice it when the game begins.

RALEIGH: You're too taken up with the game?

OSBORNE: Yes.

RALEIGH: I used to get wind up playing at school with only a few kids looking on.

OSBORNE: You feel it more when there are only a few. (*He has picked up a slip of paper from the table; suddenly he laughs.*) Look at this!

RALEIGH (*looking at it curiously*): What is it?

OSBORNE: Trotter's plan to make the time pass quickly. One hundred and forty-four little circles—one for each hour of six days. He's blacked in six already. He's six hours behind.

RALEIGH: It's rather a good idea. I like Trotter.

OSBORNE: He's a good chap.

RALEIGH: He makes things feel—natural.

OSBORNE: He's a genuine sort of chap.

RALEIGH: That's it. He's genuine. (*There is a pause. He has been filling a new pipe.*)

OSBORNE *is puffing at his old one.*

How topping—to have played for England!

OSBORNE: It *was* rather fun.

RALEIGH (*after a pause*): The Germans are really quite decent, aren't they? I mean, outside the newspapers?

OSBORNE: Yes. (*Pause.*) I remember up at Wipers we had a man shot when he was out on patrol. Just at dawn. We couldn't get him in that night. He lay out there groaning all day. Next night three of our men crawled out to get him in. It was so near the German trenches that they could have shot our fellows one by one. But, when our men began dragging the wounded man back over the rough ground, a big German officer stood up in their trenches and called out: " Carry him! "—and our fellows stood up and carried the man back and the German officer fired some lights for them to see by

RALEIGH: How topping!

OSBORNE: Next day we blew each other's trenches to blazes.

RALEIGH: It all seems rather—*silly*, doesn't it?

OSBORNE: It does, rather.

There is silence for a while.

RALEIGH: I started a letter when I came off duty last night How do we send letters?

OSBORNE: The quartermaster-sergeant takes them down after he brings rations up in the evenings.

STANHOPE *is coming slowly down the steps.* RALEIGH *rises.*

RALEIGH: I think I'll go and finish it now—if I go on duty soon.

OSBORNE: Come and write it in here. It's more cheery.

RALEIGH: It's all right, thanks; I'm quite comfortable in there. I've rigged up a sort of little table beside my bed.

OSBORNE: Righto.

RALEIGH *goes into his dug-out.* STANHOPE *is slowly taking off his equipment.*

STANHOPE: What a foul smell of bacon.

OSBORNE: Yes. We've got bacon for breakfast.

STANHOPE: So I gather. Have you told Raleigh about rifle inspection?

OSBORNE: No.

STANHOPE (*at the entrance to* RALEIGH'S *dug-out*): Raleigh!

RALEIGH (*appearing*): Yes?

STANHOPE: You inspect your platoon's rifles at nine o'clock.

RALEIGH: Oh, righto, Stanhope. (*He goes again.*)

STANHOPE (*sitting at the table*): I've arranged two wiring parties to begin at eight o'clock tonight—Corporal Burt with two men and Sergeant Smith with two. I want them to strengthen the wire all along the front.

OSBORNE: It's very weak at present.

STANHOPE: Every company leaves it for the next one to do. There're great holes blown out weeks ago.

OSBORNE: I know.

STANHOPE: Next night we'll start putting a belt of wire down both sides of us.

OSBORNE: Down the sides?

STANHOPE: Yes. We'll wire ourselves right in. If this attack comes, I'm not going to trust the companies on our sides to hold their ground.

MASON *has come in, and stands diffidently in the background.*

MASON: Would you like a nice bit o' bacon, sir?

STANHOPE: No, thanks. I'll have a cup of tea.

MASON: Right, sir.

He goes out.

STANHOPE: I've been having a good look round. We've got a strong position here—if we wire ourselves right in. The colonel's been talking to me up there.

OSBORNE: Oh. Has he been round?

STANHOPE: Yes. He says a German prisoner gave the day of attack as the 21st.

OSBORNE: That's Thursday?

STANHOPE: Yes. Today's Tuesday.

OSBORNE: That means about dawn the day after tomorrow.

STANHOPE: The second dawn from now.

There is a pause.

OSBORNE: Then it'll come while we're here.

STANHOPE: Yes. It'll come while we're here. And we shall be in the front row of the stalls.

OSBORNE: Oh, well——

In the silence that follows, MASON *enters with a cup of tea.*

MASON: Would you like a nice plate of sardines, sir?

STANHOPE: I should loathe it.

MASON: Very good, sir.

He goes out.

OSBORNE: Did the colonel have much to say?

STANHOPE: Only that when the attack comes we can't expect any help from behind. We're not to move from here. We've got to stick it.

OSBORNE: I see.

STANHOPE: We'll wire ourselves in as strongly as possible. I've got to arrange battle positions for each platoon and section this afternoon.

OSBORNE: Well, I'm glad it's coming at last. I'm sick of waiting.

STANHOPE (*looking at* TROTTER'S *chart*): What's this extraordinary affair?

OSBORNE: Trotter's plan to make the time pass by. A hundred and forty-four circles—one for each hour of six days.

STANHOPE: How many hours are there till dawn on the 21st?

OSBORNE: Goodness knows. Not many, I hope.

STANHOPE: Nearly nine o'clock now. Twenty-four till nine tomorrow; twelve till nine at night—that's thirty-six; nine till six next morning; that's forty-five altogether. (*He begins to count off forty-five circles on* TROTTER'S *chart.*)

OSBORNE: What are you going to do.

STANHOPE: At the end of the forty-fifth circle I'm going to draw a picture of Trotter being blown up in four pieces.

OSBORNE: Don't spoil his chart. It took him an hour to make that.

STANHOPE: He won't see the point. He's no imagination.

OSBORNE: I don't suppose he has.

STANHOPE: Funny not to have any imagination. Must be rather nice.

OSBORNE: A bit dull, I should think.

STANHOPE: It must be, rather. I suppose all his life Trotter feels like you and I do when we're drowsily drunk.

OSBORNE: Poor chap!

STANHOPE: I suppose if Trotter looks at that wall he just sees a brown surface. He doesn't see into the earth beyond—the worms wandering about round the stones and roots of trees. I wonder how a worm knows when it's going up or down.

OSBORNE: When it's going down I suppose the blood runs into its head and makes it throb.

STANHOPE: Worms haven't got any blood.

OSBORNE: Then I don't suppose it ever does know.

STANHOPE: Rotten if it didn't—and went on going down when it thought it was coming up.

OSBORNE: Yes. I expect that's the one thing worms dread.

STANHOPE: D'you think this life sharpens the imagination?

OSBORNE: It must.

STANHOPE: Whenever I look at anything nowadays I see right through it. Looking at you now there's your uniform—your jersey—shirt—vest—then beyond that——

OSBORNE: Let's talk about something else—croquet, or the war.

STANHOPE (*laughing*): Sorry! It's a habit that's grown on me lately—to look right through things, and on and on—till I get frightened and stop.

OSBORNE: I suppose everybody out here—*feels* more keenly.

STANHOPE: I hope so. I wondered if there was anything wrong with me. D'you ever get a sudden feeling that everything's going farther and farther away—till you're the only thing in the world—and then the world begins going away—until you're the only thing in—in the universe—and you struggle to get back—and can't?

OSBORNE: Bit of nerve strain, that's all.

STANHOPE: You don't think I'm going potty?

OSBORNE: Oh, Lord, no!

STANHOPE (*throwing back his head and laughing*): Dear old Uncle! you don't really know, do you? You just pretend you do, to make me feel all right.

OSBORNE: When people are going potty they never talk about it; they keep it to themselves.

STANHOPE: Oh, well, that's all right, then. (*There is silence for a while.*) I had that feeling this morning, standing out there in the line while the sun was rising. By the way, did you see the sunrise? Wasn't it gorgeous?

OSBORNE: Splendid—this morning.

STANHOPE: I was looking across at the Boche trenches and right beyond—not a sound or a soul; just an enormous plain, all churned up like a sea that's got muddier and muddier till it's so stiff that it can't move. You could have heard a pin drop in the quiet; yet you knew thousands of guns were hidden there, all ready cleaned and oiled—millions of bullets lying in pouches—thousands of Germans, waiting and thinking. Then, gradually, that feeling came——

OSBORNE: I never knew the sun could rise in so many ways till I came out here. Green, and pink, and red, and blue, and grey. Extraordinary, isn't it?

STANHOPE: Yes.   Hi!   Mason!

MASON (*outside*): Yessir!

STANHOPE: Bring some mugs and a bottle of whisky.

MASON: Yessir.

OSBORNE (*smiling*): So early in the morning?

STANHOPE: Just a spot.   It's damn cold in here.

OSBORNE (*turning over the pages of a magazine*): This show at the Hippodrome has been running a long time.

STANHOPE: What?   *Zig-zag?*

OSBORNE: Yes.   George Robey's in it.

STANHOPE: Harper saw it on leave.   Says it's damn good. Robey's pricelessly funny.

MASON *brings whisky and mugs and water.*

OSBORNE: Wish I'd seen a show on leave.

STANHOPE: D'you mean to say you didn't go to any shows?

OSBORNE (*laughing*): No.   I spent all the time in the garden, making a rockery.   In the evenings I used to sit and smoke and read—and my wife used to knit socks and play the piano a bit.   We pretended there wasn't any war at all—till my two youngsters made me help in a tin-soldier battle on the floor.

STANHOPE: Poor old Uncle!   You can't get away from it, can you?

OSBORNE: I wish I knew how to fight a battle like those boys of mine.   You ought to have seen the way they lured my men under the sofa and mowed them down.

STANHOPE (*laughing and helping himself to a drink*): You going to have one?

OSBORNE: Not now, thanks.

STANHOPE: You go on duty at eleven, don't you?

OSBORNE: Yes.   I relieve Trotter.

STANHOPE: Raleigh better go on at one o'clock and stay with you for an hour.   Then he can stay on alone till four.   Hibbert relieves him at four.

OSBORNE: Righto.

STANHOPE: What's Raleigh doing now?

OSBORNE: Finishing a letter.

STANHOPE: Did you tell him?

OSBORNE: About what?

STANHOPE: Censorship.

OSBORNE: You don't mean that seriously?

STANHOPE: Mean it? Of course I mean it.

OSBORNE: You can't do that.

STANHOPE: Officially I'm supposed to read all your letters. Damn it all, Uncle! Imagine yourself in my place—a letter going away from here—from that boy——

OSBORNE: He'll say nothing—rotten—about you.

STANHOPE: You think so? (*There is a pause.*) I heard you go on duty last night. After you'd gone, I got up. I was feeling bad. I forgot Raleigh was out there with Trotter. I'd forgotten all about him. I was sleepy. I just knew something beastly had happened. Then he came in with Trotter—and looked at me. After coming in out of the night air, this place must have reeked of candle-grease, and rats—and whisky. One thing a boy like that can't stand is a smell that isn't fresh. He looked at me as if I'd hit him between the eyes—as if I'd spat on him——

OSBORNE: You imagine things.

STANHOPE (*laughing*): Imagine things! No need to imagine!

OSBORNE: Why can't you treat him like any other youngster?

RALEIGH *comes in from his dug-out with a letter in his hand. He stops short as he notices the abrupt silence that follows his entry.*

RALEIGH: I'm sorry.

OSBORNE: It's all right, Raleigh. Going to inspect rifles?

RALEIGH: Yes.

OSBORNE: You needn't bother if the wood's a bit dirty—just the barrels and magazines and all the metal parts.

RALEIGH: Righto.

OSBORNE: See there's plenty of oil on it. And look at the ammunition in the men's pouches.

RALEIGH: Right. (*He crosses towards the door and turns.*) Where do we put the letters to be collected?

OSBORNE: Oh, just on the table.

RALEIGH: Thanks. (*He begins to lick the flap of the envelope.*)

STANHOPE (*in a quiet voice*): You leave it open.

RALEIGH (*surprised*): Open?

STANHOPE: Yes. I have to censor all letters.

RALEIGH (*stammering*): Oh, but—I haven't said anything about —where we are——

STANHOPE: It's the rule that letters must be read.

RALEIGH (*nervously*): Oh, I—I didn't realise that. (*He stands embarrassed; then gives a short laugh.*) I—I think—I'll just leave it, then. (*He unbuttons his tunic pocket to put the letter away.*)

STANHOPE, *rises, slowly crosses and faces* RALEIGH.

STANHOPE: Give me that letter!

RALEIGH (*astonished*): But—Dennis——

STANHOPE (*trembling*): Give me that letter!

RALEIGH: But it's—it's private. I didn't know——

STANHOPE: D'you understand an order? Give me that letter!

RALEIGH: But I tell you—there's nothing——

STANHOPE *clutches* RALEIGH's *wrist and tears the letter from his hand.*

Dennis—I'm——

STANHOPE: Don't "Dennis" me! Stanhope's my name! You're not at school! Go and inspect your rifles!

RALEIGH *stands in amazement at the foot of the steps.*

(*Shouting*)   D'you understand an order?

For a moment RALEIGH *stares wide-eyed at* STANHOPE, *who is trembling and breathing heavily, then almost in a whisper he says:* "Right," *and goes quietly up the narrow steps.*

STANHOPE *turns towards the table.*

OSBORNE: Good heavens, Stanhope!

STANHOPE (*wheeling furiously on* OSBORNE): Look here, Osborne, I'm commanding this company. I ask for advice when I want it!

OSBORNE: Very well.

STANHOPE *sinks down at the table with the letter in his hand. There is silence for a moment. Then he throws the letter on the table and rests his head between his hands.*

STANHOPE: Oh, God! I don't want to read the blasted thing!

OSBORNE: You'll let it go, then?

STANHOPE: I don't care.   (*There is a pause.*)

OSBORNE: Shall I glance through it—for you?

STANHOPE: If you like.

OSBORNE: I don't *want* to.

STANHOPE: You better.   I can't.

OSBORNE *takes the letter from the table and opens it.* STANHOPE *sits with his head in his hand, digging a magazine with a pencil. After a while,* OSBORNE *glances up at* STANHOPE.

OSBORNE: D'you want to hear?

STANHOPE: I suppose I better know.

OSBORNE: He begins with a description of his getting here— he doesn't mention the names of any places.

STANHOPE: What does he say then?

OSBORNE: The last piece is about you.

STANHOPE: Go on.

OSBORNE (*reading*): He says: " And now I come to the great news. I reported at Battalion Headquarters, and the colonel looked in a little book, and said, ' You report to " C " Company—Captain Stanhope.' Can't you imagine what I felt? I was taken along some trenches and shown a dug-out. There was an awfully nice officer there—quite old—with grey hair "—(OSBORNE *clears his throat*)—" and then later Dennis came in. He looked tired, but that's because he works so frightfully hard, and because of the responsibility. Then I went on duty in the front line, and a sergeant told me all about Dennis. He said that Dennis is the finest officer in the battalion, and the men simply love him. He hardly ever sleeps in the dug-out; he's always up in the front line with the men, cheering them on with jokes, and making them keen about things, like he did the kids at school. I'm awfully proud to think he's my friend."

There is silence. STANHOPE *has not moved while* OSBORNE *has read.*

That's all. (*Pause.*) Shall I stick it down?

STANHOPE *sits with lowered head. He murmurs something that sounds like* " Yes, please." *He rises heavily and crosses to the shadows by* OSBORNE'S *bed.*

The sun is shining quite brightly in the trench outside.

THE CURTAIN FALLS

SCENE 2

Afternoon on the same day. The sunlight has gone from the dug-out floor, but still shines brightly in the trench.

STANHOPE *is lying on his bed reading by the light of a candle on the table beside him. A burly* FIGURE *comes groping down the steps and stands blinking in the shadows of the dug-out. A huge man, with a heavy black moustache, a fat red face, and massive chin.*

STANHOPE *puts the magazine down, rises, and sits up to the table.*

STANHOPE: I want to talk with you, sergeant-major.

S.-M. (*standing stolidly by the steps*): Yes, sir?

STANHOPE: Sit down. Have a whisky?

S.-M. (*a suspicion of brightness in his voice*): Thank you, sir.

The SERGEANT-MAJOR *diffidently takes a small tot.*

STANHOPE: I say. You won't taste that. Take a proper one.

S.-M.: Well—sir——

STANHOPE *reaches over, helps the* SERGEANT-MAJOR *to a large tot, and takes one himself.*

Turning chilly again, sir. Quite warm this morning.

STANHOPE: Yes.

S.-M.: Well, here's your very good health, sir. (*He raises his glass and drinks.*)

STANHOPE: Cheero. (*He puts down his glass and abruptly changes his tone.*) Now, look here, sergeant-major. We must expect this attack on Thursday morning, at dawn. That's the second dawn from now.

The SERGEANT-MAJOR *takes a very dirty little notebook from his pocket and jots down notes with a very small stub of pencil.*

S.-M.: Thursday morning. Very good, sir.

STANHOPE: We're to hold these trenches, and no man's to move from here.

S.-M.: Very good, sir.

STANHOPE: It may happen that companies on our sides will give way, leaving our flanks exposed; so I want a screen of wire put down both flanks till it meets the wire in the support line.

S.-M. (*writing hurriedly*): Both flanks—yes, sir.

STANHOPE: When the attack begins, I shall take charge of the left, and Mr. Osborne the right. You will be with Mr. Osborne, and Sergeant Baker with me; 9 and 10 Platoons will move over here (*he points out the position on the trench map*); 11 and 12 Platoons to the left.

S.-M.: I see, sir.

STANHOPE: Is there anything you're not clear about?

S.-M. (*looking at his notes*): Seems all clear, sir.

STANHOPE: Anything you want to know?

S.-M.: Well, sir (*clears his throat*)—when the attack comes, of course, we beat 'em off—but what if they keep on attacking?

STANHOPE: Then we keep on beating them off.

S.-M.: Yes, sir. But what I mean is—they're bound to make a big thing of it.

STANHOPE (*cheerily*): Oh, I think they will!

S.-M.: Well, then, sir. If they don't get through the first day, they'll attack the next day and the next——

STANHOPE: They're bound to.

S.-M.: Then oughtn't we to fix up something about, well (*he gropes for the right words*)—er—falling back?

STANHOPE: There's no need to—you see, this company's a lot better than " A " and " B " Companies on either side of us.

S.-M.: Quite, sir.

STANHOPE: Well, then, if anyone breaks, " A " and " B " will break before we do. As long as we stick here when the other companies have given way, we can fire into the Boche as they try and get through the gaps on our sides—we'll make a hell of a mess of them. We might delay the advance a whole day.

S.-M. (*diffidently*): Yes, sir, but what 'appens when the Boche 'as all got round the back of us?

STANHOPE: Then we advance and win the war.

S.-M. (*pretending to make a note*): Win the war. Very good, sir.

STANHOPE: But you understand exactly what I mean, sergeant-major. Our orders are to stick here. If you're told to stick where you are you don't make plans to retire.

S.-M.: Quite, sir.

OSBORNE's *voice is calling down the steps.* SERGEANT-MAJOR *rises.*

OSBORNE: Are you there, Stanhope?

STANHOPE (*rising quickly*): Yes. What's the matter?

OSBORNE: The colonel's up here. Wants to see you——

STANHOPE: Oh, right, I'll come up.

COLONEL (*from above*): All right, Stanhope—I'll come down.

S.-M. (*who has risen*): Anything more, sir?

STANHOPE: I don't think so. I'll see you at stand-to this evening.

S.-M.: Very good, sir.

He stands back a pace and salutes STANHOPE *smartly.* STANHOPE's *eye falls on the* SERGEANT-MAJOR's *nearly finished drink on the table. He points to it.*

STANHOPE: Hoy! What about that?

S.-M.: Thank you, sir. (*He finishes the drink.*)

   The COLONEL *comes down the steps.*

COLONEL: Good morning, sergeant-major.

S.-M.: Good morning, sir.

   The SERGEANT-MAJOR *goes up the steps.*

STANHOPE: Hullo, sir!

COLONEL: Hullo, Stanhope! (*He sniffs.*) Strong smell of bacon.

STANHOPE: Yes, sir. We had some bacon for breakfast.

COLONEL: Hangs about, doesn't it?

STANHOPE: Yes, sir. Clings to the walls.

COLONEL: Lovely day.

STANHOPE: Splendid, sir.

COLONEL: Spring's coming. (*There is a pause.*) I'm glad you're alone. I've got some rather serious news.

STANHOPE: I'm sorry to hear that, sir. Will you have a drink?

COLONEL: Well, thanks—just a spot.

   STANHOPE *mixes a drink for the* COLONEL *and himself.*

   Here's luck.

STANHOPE: Cheero, sir. (*Bringing forward a box.*) Sit down, sir.

COLONEL: Thanks.

STANHOPE: What's the news, sir?

COLONEL: The brigadier came to see me this morning. (*He pauses.*) It seems almost certain the attack's to come on Thursday morning. They've got information from more than one source—but they don't know where it's going to fall the hardest. The Boche began relieving his front-line troops yesterday. They're bound to put in certain regiments where they intend to make the hardest push——

STANHOPE: Naturally——

COLONEL: And the general wants us to make a raid to find out who's come into the line opposite here.

   There is a pause.

STANHOPE: I see. When?

COLONEL: As soon as possible. He said tonight.

STANHOPE: Oh, but that's absurd!

COLONEL: I told him so. I said the earliest would be tomorrow afternoon. A surprise daylight raid under a smoke screen from the trench-mortar people. I think daylight best. There's not much moon now, and it's vitally important to get hold of a Boche or two.

STANHOPE: Quite.

COLONEL: I suggest sending two officers and ten men. Quite enough for the purpose. Just opposite here there's only seventy yards of No Man's Land. Tonight the trench-mortars can blow a hole in the Boche wire and you can cut a hole in yours. Harrison of the trench-mortars is coming in to dinner with me this evening to discuss everything. I'd like you to come too. Eight o'clock suit you?

STANHOPE: Very good, sir.

COLONEL: I'll leave you to select the men.

STANHOPE: You want me to go with them, sir?

COLONEL: Oh, no, Stanhope. I—I can't let you go. No. I want one officer to direct the raid and one to make the dash in and collar some Boche.

STANHOPE: Who do you suggest, sir?

COLONEL: Well, I suggest Osborne, for one. He's a very level-headed chap. He can direct it.

STANHOPE: And who else?

COLONEL: Well, there's Trotter—but he's a bit fat, isn't he? Not much good at dashing in?

STANHOPE: No. D'you suggest Hibbert?

COLONEL: Well, what do *you* think of Hibbert?

STANHOPE: I don't think so.

COLONEL: No.

There is a pause.

STANHOPE: Why not send a good sergeant, sir?

COLONEL: No. I don't think a sergeant. The men expect officers to lead a raid.

STANHOPE: Yes.   There is that.

COLONEL: As a matter of fact, Stanhope, I'm thinking of that youngster I sent up to you last night.

STANHOPE: Raleigh?

COLONEL: Yes.   Just the type.   Plenty of guts——

STANHOPE: He's awfully new to it all——

COLONEL: All to the good.   His nerves are sound.

STANHOPE: It's rotten to send a fellow who's only just arrived.

COLONEL: Well, who else is there?   I could send an officer from another company——

STANHOPE (*quickly*): Oh, Lord, no.   We'll do it.

COLONEL: Then I suggest Osborne to direct the raid and Raleigh to make the dash—with ten good men.   We'll meet Harrison at supper and arrange the smoke bombs—and blowing a hole in the wire.   You select the men and talk to Osborne and Raleigh about it in the meantime.

STANHOPE: Very well, sir.

COLONEL: Better send Osborne and Raleigh down to me in the morning to talk things over.   Or better still!—I'll come up here first thing tomorrow morning.

STANHOPE: Right, sir.

COLONEL: It's all a damn nuisance; but, after all—it's necessary.

STANHOPE: I suppose it is.

COLONEL: Well, so long, Stanhope.   I'll see you at eight o'clock. Do you like fish?

STANHOPE: Fish, sir?

COLONEL: Yes.   We've had some fresh fish sent up from rail head for supper tonight.

STANHOPE: Splendid, sir!

COLONEL: Whiting, I think it is.

STANHOPE: Good!

COLONEL: Well, bye-bye.

The COLONEL *goes up the steps.*

STANHOPE *stands watching for a moment, then turns and walks slowly to the table.*

HIBBERT *comes quietly into the dug-out from the tunnel leading from his sleeping quarters.*

STANHOPE: Hullo! I thought you were asleep.

HIBBERT: I just wanted a word with you, Stanhope.

STANHOPE: Fire away.

HIBBERT: This neuralgia of mine. I'm awfully sorry. I'm afraid I can't stick it any longer——

STANHOPE: I know. It's rotten, isn't it? I've got it like hell——-

HIBBERT (*taken aback*): *You* have?

STANHOPE: Had it for weeks.

HIBBERT: Well, I'm sorry, Stanhope. It's no good. I've tried damned hard; but I must go down——

STANHOPE: Go down—where?

HIBBERT: Why, go sick—go down the line. I must go into hospital and have some kind of treatment.

There is a silence for a moment. STANHOPE *is looking at* HIBBERT— *till* HIBBERT *turns away and walks towards his dug-out.*

I'll go right along now, I think——

STANHOPE (*quietly*): You're going to stay here.

HIBBERT: I'm going down to see the doctor. He'll send me to hospital when he understands——

STANHOPE: I've seen the doctor. I saw him this morning. He won't send you to hospital, Hibbert; he'll send you back here. He promised me he would. (*There is silence.*) So you can save yourself a walk.

HIBBERT (*fiercely*): What the hell——!

STANHOPE: Stop that!

HIBBERT: I've a perfect right to go sick if I want to. The men can—why can't an officer?

STANHOPE: No man's sent down unless he's very ill. There's nothing wrong with you, Hibbert. The German attack's on Thursday; almost for certain. You're going to stay here and see it through with the rest of us.

HIBBERT (*hysterically*): I tell you, I *can't*—the pain's nearly send-ing me mad. I'm going; I've got all my stuff packed. I'm going now—*you* can't stop me!

He goes excitedly into the dug-out. STANHOPE *walks slowly towards the steps, turns, and undoes the flap of his revolver holster. He takes out his revolver, and stands casually examining it.*

HIBBERT *returns with his pack slung on his back and a walking-stick in his hand. He pauses at the sight of* STANHOPE *by the steps.*

HIBBERT: Let's get by, Stanhope.

STANHOPE: You're going to stay here and do your job.

HIBBERT: Haven't I *told* you? I *can't*! Don't you understand? Let—let me get by.

STANHOPE: Now look here, Hibbert. I've got a lot of work to do and no time to waste. Once and for all, you're going to stay here and see it through with the rest of us.

HIBBERT: I shall die of this pain if I don't go!

STANHOPE: Better die of the pain than be shot for deserting.

HIBBERT (*in a low voice*): What do you mean?

STANHOPE: You know what I mean——

HIBBERT: I've a right to see the doctor!

STANHOPE: Good God! Don't you understand!—he'll send you back here. Dr. Preston's never let a shirker pass him yet—and he's not going to start now—two days before the attack——

HIBBERT (*pleadingly*): Stanhope—if you only *knew* how awful I feel—— Please do let me go by——

He walks slowly round behind STANHOPE. STANHOPE *turns and thrusts him roughly back. With a lightning movement* HIBBERT *raises his stick and strikes blindly at* STANHOPE, *who catches the stick, tears it from* HIBBERT's *hands, smashes it across his knee, and throws it on the ground.*

STANHOPE: God!— you little swine. You know what that means—don't you? Striking a superior officer!

There is silence. STANHOPE *takes hold of his revolver as it swings from its lanyard.* HIBBERT *stands quivering in front of* STANHOPE.

Never mind, though. I won't have you shot for that——

HIBBERT: Let me go——

STANHOPE: If you went, I'd have you shot—for deserting. It's a hell of a disgrace—to die like that. I'd rather spare you the disgrace. I give you half a minute to think. You either stay here and try and be a man—or you try to get out of that door—to desert. If you do that, there's going to be an accident. D'you understand? I'm fiddling with my revolver, d'you see?—cleaning it—and it's going off by accident. It often happens out here. It's going off, and it's going to shoot you between the eyes.

HIBBERT (*in a whisper*): You daren't——

STANHOPE: You don't deserve to be shot by accident—but I'd save you the disgrace of the other way—I give you half a minute to decide. (*He holds up his wrist to look at his watch.*) Half a minute from now——

There is silence; a few seconds go by. Suddenly HIBBERT *bursts into a high-pitched laugh.*

HIBBERT: Go on, then, shoot! You won't let me go to hospital. I swear I'll never go into those trenches again. Shoot!—and thank God——

STANHOPE (*with his eyes on his watch*): Fifteen more seconds——-

HIBBERT: Go on! I'm ready——

STANHOPE: Ten. (*He looks up at* HIBBERT, *who has closed his eyes.*) Five.

Again STANHOPE *looks up. After a moment he quietly drops his revolver into its holster and steps towards* HIBBERT, *who stands with lowered head and eyes tightly screwed up, his arms stretched stiffly by his sides, his hands tightly clutching the edges of his tunic. Gently* STANHOPE *places his hands on* HIBBERT'S *shoulders.* HIBBERT *starts violently and gives a little cry. He opens his eyes and stares vacantly into* STANHOPE'S *face.* STANHOPE *is smiling.*

STANHOPE: Good man, Hibbert. I liked the way you stuck that.

HIBBERT (*hoarsely*): Why didn't you shoot?

STANHOPE: Stay here, old chap—and see it through——

HIBBERT *stands trembling, trying to speak. Suddenly he breaks down and cries.* STANHOPE *takes his hands from his shoulders and turns away.*

HIBBERT: Stanhope! I've tried like hell—I swear I have. Ever since I came out here I've hated and loathed it. Every sound up there makes me all—cold and sick. I'm different to—to the others—you don't understand. It's got worse and worse, and now I can't bear it any longer. I'll never go up those steps again—into the line—with the men looking at me—and knowing—I'd rather die here. (*He is sitting on* STANHOPE'S *bed, crying without effort to restrain himself.*)

STANHOPE (*pouring out a whisky*): Try a drop of this, old chap——

HIBBERT: No, thanks.

STANHOPE: Go on. Drink it.

HIBBERT *takes the mug and drinks.*

STANHOPE *sits down beside* HIBBERT *and puts an arm round his shoulder.*

I know what you feel, Hibbert. I've known all along——

HIBBERT: How *can* you know?

STANHOPE: Because I feel the same—exactly the same! Every little noise up there makes me feel—just as you feel. Why didn't you tell me instead of talking about neuralgia? We *all* feel like you do sometimes, if you only knew. I hate and loathe it all. Sometimes I feel I could just lie down on this bed and pretend I was paralysed or something—and couldn't move—and just lie there till I died—or was dragged away.

HIBBERT: I can't bear to go up into those awful trenches again——

STANHOPE: When are you due to go on?

HIBBERT: Quite soon. At four.

STANHOPE: Shall we go on together? We know how we both feel now. Shall we see if we can stick it together?

HIBBERT: I can't——

STANHOPE: Supposing I said *I* can't—supposing we *all* say we can't—what would happen then?

HIBBERT: I don't care. What does it matter? It's all so—so beastly—nothing matters——

STANHOPE: Supposing the worst happened—supposing we were

knocked right out. Think of all the chaps who've gone already. It can't be very lonely there—with all those fellows. Sometimes I think it's lonelier here. (*He pauses.*)

HIBBERT *is sitting quietly now, his eyes roving vacantly in front of him.*

Just go and have a quiet rest. Then we'll go out together.

HIBBERT: Do please let me go, Stanhope——

STANHOPE: If you went—and left Osborne and Trotter and Raleigh and all those men up there to do your work—could you ever look a man straight in the face again—in all your life? (*There is silence again.*) You may be wounded. Then you can go home and feel proud—and if you're killed you—you won't have to stand this hell any more. I might have fired just now. If I had you would have been dead now. But you're still alive—with a straight fighting chance of coming through. Take the chance, old chap, and stand in with Osborne and Trotter and Raleigh. Don't you think it worth standing in with men like that?—when you know they all feel like you do—in their hearts—and just go on sticking it because they know it's—it's the only thing a decent man can do. (*Again there is silence.*) What about it?

HIBBERT: I'll—I'll try——

STANHOPE: Good man!

HIBBERT: You—you won't say anything, Stanhope—about this?

STANHOPE: If you promise not to tell anyone what a blasted funk *I* am.

HIBBERT (*with a little laugh*): No.

STANHOPE: Splendid! Now go and have ten minutes' rest and a smoke—then we'll go up together and hold each other's hands—and jump every time a rat squeaks.

HIBBERT *rises and blows his nose.*

We've all got a good fighting chance. *I* mean to come through—don't you?

HIBBERT: Yes. Rather. (*He goes timidly towards his dug-out, and turns at the doorway.*) It's awfully decent of you, Stanhope—

STANHOPE *is pouring himself out a whisky.*

and thanks most awfully for——

STANHOPE: That's all right.

HIBBERT *goes away.*

STANHOPE *takes a drink and sits down at the table to write.*

MASON *comes in.*

MASON: Will you have a nice cup of tea, sir?

STANHOPE: Can you guarantee it's nice?

MASON: Well, sir—it's a bit oniony, but that's only because of the saucepan.

STANHOPE: In other words, it's onion soup with tea-leaves in it?

MASON: Not till dinner-time, sir.

STANHOPE: All right, Mason. Bring two cups of onion tea. One for Mr. Hibbert.

MASON: Very good, sir.

Going towards the door, he meets OSBORNE *coming in.*

Will you have a nice cup of tea, sir?

OSBORNE: Please, Mason—and plenty of bread and butter and strawberry jam.

MASON: Very good, sir.

STANHOPE: Well, Uncle—how are things going on up there?

OSBORNE: Two lonely rifle grenades came over just now.

STANHOPE: I heard them. Where did they pitch?

OSBORNE: Just over the front line on the left. Otherwise nothing doing.

Pause.

STANHOPE: The colonel's been talking to me.

OSBORNE: About the attack?

STANHOPE: Partly. We've got to make a raid, Uncle.

OSBORNE: Oh? When?

STANHOPE: Tomorrow afternoon. Under a smoke screen. Two officers and ten men.

OSBORNE: Who's going?

STANHOPE: You and Raleigh.

CHARLESTON ACADEMY
ENGLISH DEPARTMENT

Pause.

OSBORNE: Oh. (*There is another pause.*) Why Raleigh?

STANHOPE: The colonel picked you to direct and Raleigh to dash in.

OSBORNE: I see.

STANHOPE: The brigade wants to know who's opposite here.

OSBORNE: Tomorrow? What time?

STANHOPE: I suggest about five o'clock. A little before dusk——

OSBORNE: I see.

STANHOPE: I'm damn sorry.

OSBORNE: That's all right, old chap.

STANHOPE: I'm dining with the colonel to arrange everything. Then I'll come back and go through it with you.

OSBORNE: Where do we raid from?

STANHOPE: Out of the sap on our left. Straight across.

OSBORNE: Where's the map?

STANHOPE: Here we are. Look. Straight across to this sentry post of the Boche. Sixty yards. Tonight we'll lay out a guiding tape as far as possible. After dark the toch-emmas[1] are going to break the Boche wire and we'll cut a passage in ours.

OSBORNE: Will you fix up the men who are to go?

STANHOPE: Are you keen on any special men?

OSBORNE: Can I take a corporal?

STANHOPE: Sure.

OSBORNE: May I have young Crooks?

STANHOPE: Righto.

OSBORNE: You'll ask for volunteers, I suppose?

STANHOPE: Yes. I'll see the sergeant-major and get him to go round for names.

[1] Toch-emmas—signallers need to be able to identify letters of the alphabet by words, *e.g.*, A for apple, B for beautiful. Toch emma stood for TM, and TM for trench mortars.

He crosses to the doorway as MASON *comes in with the tea.*

MASON: Your tea, sir!

STANHOPE: Keep it hot, Mason.

MASON: Will you take this cup, Mr. Osborne?

STANHOPE: Take the other in to Mr. Hibbert, in there.

MASON: Very good, sir.

He goes into HIBBERT'S *dug-out.*

STANHOPE: Shan't be long, Uncle.

He goes up the steps.

OSBORNE: Righto.

MASON returns.

MASON: Will you have cut bread and butter—or shall I bring the loaf, sir?

OSBORNE: Cut it, Mason, please.

MASON: Just bringing the jam separately?

OSBORNE: Yes.

MASON: Very good, sir.

MASON goes out.

OSBORNE *takes a small leather bound book from his pocket, opens it at a marker, and begins to read.*

TROTTER *appears from the sleeping dug-out looking very sleepy.*

TROTTER: Tea ready?

OSBORNE: Yes.

TROTTER: Why's Hibbert got his tea in there?

OSBORNE: I don't know.

TROTTER (*rubbing his eyes*): Oh, Lord, I do feel frowsy. 'Ad a fine sleep, though.

MASON brings more tea and a pot of jam.

MASON: Bread just coming, sir. 'Ere's the strawberry jam, sir.

TROTTER (*reciting*):

" ' Tell me, mother, what is that
    That looks like strawberry jam?'
    ' Hush, hush, my dear; 'tis only Pa
    Run over by a tram—' "

OSBORNE: The colonel came here while you were asleep.

TROTTER: Oh?

OSBORNE: We've got to make a raid tomorrow afternoon.

TROTTER: Oh, Lord!   What—all of us?

OSBORNE: Two officers and ten men.

TROTTER: Who's got to do it?

OSBORNE: Raleigh and I.

TROTTER: Raleigh!

OSBORNE: Yes.

TROTTER: But 'e's only just come!

OSBORNE: Apparently that's the reason.

TROTTER: And you're going too?

OSBORNE: Yes.

TROTTER: Let's 'ear all about it.

OSBORNE: I know nothing yet. Except that it's got to be done.

TROTTER: What a damn nuisance!

OSBORNE: It is, rather.

TROTTER: I reckon the Boche are all ready waiting for it. Did
    you 'ear about the raid just south of 'ere the other night?

OSBORNE: Nothing much.

TROTTER: The trench-mortars go and knock an 'ole in the
    Boche wire to let our fellers through—and in the night the
    Boche went out and tied bits o' red rag on each side of the
    'ole!

OSBORNE: Yes.   I heard about that.

TROTTER: And even then our fellers 'ad to make the raid. It
    was murder. Doesn't this tea taste of onions?

OSBORNE: It does a bit.

TROTTER: Pity Mason don't clean 'is pots better.

MASON *brings some bread on a plate.*

This tea tastes of onions.

MASON: I'm sorry, sir. Onions do 'ave such a way of cropping up again.

TROTTER: Yes, but we 'aven't 'ad onions for days!

MASON: I know, sir. That's what makes it so funny.

TROTTER: Well, you better do something about it.

MASON: I'll look into it, sir.

He goes out.

OSBORNE *and* TROTTER *prepare themselves slices of bread and jam.*

TROTTER: Joking apart. It's damn ridiculous making a raid when the Boche are expecting it.

OSBORNE: We're not doing it for fun.

TROTTER: I know.

OSBORNE: You might avoid talking to Raleigh about it.

TROTTER: Why? How do you mean?

OSBORNE: There's no need to tell him it's murder——

TROTTER: Oh, Lord! no. (*He pauses.*) I'm sorry 'e's got to go. 'E's a nice young feller——

OSBORNE *turns to his book. There is silence.*

What are you reading?

OSBORNE (*wearily*). Oh, just a book.

TROTTER: What's the title?

OSBORNE (*showing him the cover*): Ever read it?

TROTTER (*leaning over and reading the cover*): *Alice's Adventures in Wonderland*— why, that's a kid's book!

OSBORNE: Yes.

TROTTER: You aren't *reading* it?

OSBORNE: Yes.

TROTTER: What—a *kid's* book.

OSBORNE: Haven't you read it?

TROTTER (*scornfully*): No!

OSBORNE: You ought to. (*Reads*):

" How doth the little crocodile
        Improve his shining tail,
   And pour the waters of the Nile
        On every golden scale?

" How cheerfully he seems to grin
        And neatly spread his claws,
   And welcomes little fishes in
        With gently smiling jaws! "

TROTTER (*after a moment's thought*): I don't see no point in that.

OSBORNE (*wearily*): Exactly. That's just the point.

TROTTER (*looking curiously at* OSBORNE): You *are* a funny chap!

   STANHOPE *returns.*

STANHOPE: The sergeant-major's getting volunteers.

OSBORNE: Good!

TROTTER: Sorry to 'ear about the raid, skipper.

STANHOPE (*shortly*): So am I. What do you make the time?

TROTTER: Just on four.

   MASON *brings in more tea.*

STANHOPE (*taking the mug of tea*): Was Hibbert asleep when you came out of there?

TROTTER: No. 'E was just lying on 'is bed, smoking.

STANHOPE (*going to the sleeping dug-out*): Hibbert!

HIBBERT (*coming out*): I'm ready, Stanhope.

STANHOPE: Had some tea?

HIBBERT: Yes, thanks.

TROTTER: I reckon Raleigh'll be glad to be relieved. Rotten being on dooty for the first time alone.

OSBORNE: I don't think he minds.

STANHOPE: I shall be up there some time, Uncle.

OSBORNE: I say, why don't you have a rest?—you've been on the go all day.

STANHOPE: There's too much to do. This raid's going to upset the arrangements of the wiring party tonight. Can't have men out there while the toch-emmas are blowing holes in the

Boche wire. (*He drinks up his tea.*) Ready, Hibbert? Come on, my lad.

STANHOPE *and* HIBBERT *leave the dug-out together.* TROTTER *looks after them curiously, and turns to* OSBORNE.

TROTTER: Can't understand that little feller, can you?

OSBORNE: Who?

TROTTER: Why, 'Ibbert. D'you see 'is eyes? All red. 'E told me in there 'e'd got 'ay-fever.

OSBORNE: Rotten thing, hay-fever.

TROTTER: If you ask me, 'e's been crying——

OSBORNE *is writing at the table.*

OSBORNE: Maybe.

TROTTER: Funny little bloke, isn't 'e?

OSBORNE: Yes, I say—d'you mind? I just want to get a letter off.

TROTTER: Oh, sorry. They 'aven't collected the letters yet, then?

OSBORNE: Not yet.

TROTTER: I'll get one off to my old lady. (*He goes towards his dug-out.*) She's wrote and asked if I've got fleas.

OSBORNE: Have you?

TROTTER (*gently rotating his shoulders*): I wish it *was* fleas.

TROTTER *goes into his dug-out;* OSBORNE *continues his letter.*

RALEIGH *comes down the steps from the trench.*

RALEIGH (*excitedly*): I say, Stanhope's told me about the raid.

OSBORNE: Has he?

RALEIGH: Just you and me, isn't it—and ten men?

OSBORNE: Yes, tomorrow. Just before dusk. Under a smoke cloud.

RALEIGH: I say—it's most frightfully exciting!

OSBORNE: We shall know more about it after Stanhope sees the colonel tonight.

RALEIGH: Were you and I picked—specially?

OSBORNE: Yes.

RALEIGH: I say!

THE CURTAIN FALLS

ACT III

SCENE I

The following day, towards sunset. The earth wall of the trench outside glows with a light that slowly fades with the sinking sun.

STANHOPE *is alone, wandering to and fro across the dug-out. He looks up the steps for a moment, crosses to the table, and glances down at the map. He looks anxiously at his watch, and, going to the servant's dug-out, calls:*

STANHOPE: Mason!

MASON (*outside*): Yessir!

STANHOPE: Are you making the coffee?

MASON: Yessir!

STANHOPE: Make it hot and strong. Ready in five minutes. I'll call when it's wanted.

MASON: Very good, sir.

Again STANHOPE *wanders restlessly to and fro. The* COLONEL *comes down the steps.*

COLONEL: Everything ready?

STANHOPE: Yes, sir. (*There is silence.*) You've no news, then?

COLONEL: I'm afraid not. It's got to be done.

STANHOPE (*after a pause*): I see.

COLONEL: The brigadier says the Boche did the same thing just south of here the other day.

STANHOPE: I know; but didn't you suggest we altered our plans and made a surprise raid farther **up** the line after dark?

COLONEL: Yes. I suggested that.

STANHOPE: What did he say?

COLONEL: He said the present arrangements have got to stand.

STANHOPE: But surely he must realise——?

COLONEL (*impatiently breaking in*): Look here, Stanhope, I've done all I can, but my report's got to be at headquarters by seven this evening. If we wait till it's dark we shall be too late.

STANHOPE: Why seven?

COLONEL: They've got some conference to arrange the placing of reserves.

STANHOPE: They can't have it later because of dinner, I suppose.

COLONEL: Lots of raids have taken place along the line today. With the attack tomorrow morning, headquarters naturally want all the information they can get as early as possible.

STANHOPE: Meanwhile the Boche are sitting over there with a dozen machine-guns trained on that hole—waiting for our fellows to come.

COLONEL: Well, I can't disobey orders.

STANHOPE: Why didn't the trench-mortars blow a dozen holes in different places—so the Boche wouldn't know which we were going to use?

COLONEL: It took three hours to blow that one. How could they blow a dozen in the time? It's no good worrying about that now. It's too late. Where's Osborne and Raleigh?

STANHOPE: They're up in the sap, having a last look round. What d'you make the time, sir?

COLONEL: Exactly nineteen minutes to.

STANHOPE: I'm thirty seconds behind you.

COLONEL: Funny. We checked this morning.

STANHOPE: Still, it's near enough. We shan't go till the smoke blows across.

COLONEL: The smoke ought to blow across nicely. The wind's just right. I called on the trench-mortars on the way up. Everything's ready. They'll drop the bombs thirty yards to the right.

STANHOPE: Are you going to stay here?

COLONEL: I'll watch from the trench just above, I think. Bring the prisoners straight back here. We'll question them right away.

STANHOPE: Why not take them straight down to your head-quarters?

COLONEL: Well, the Boche are bound to shell pretty heavily. I don't want the risk of the prisoners being knocked out before we've talked to them.

STANHOPE: All right. I'll have them brought back here.

There is a pause. The COLONEL *sucks hard at his pipe.* STANHOPE *roves restlessly about, smoking a cigarette.*

COLONEL: It's no good getting depressed. After all, it's only sixty yards. The Boche'll be firing into a blank fog. Osborne's a cool, level-headed chap, and Raleigh's the very man to dash in. You've picked good men to follow them?

STANHOPE: The best. All youngsters. Strong, keen chaps.

COLONEL: Good. (*Another pause.*) You know quite well I'd give anything to cancel the beastly affair.

STANHOPE: I know you would, sir.

COLONEL: Have these red rags on the wire upset the men at all?

STANHOPE: It's hard to tell. They naturally take it as a joke. They say the rags are just what they want to show them the way through the gap.

COLONEL: That's the spirit. Stanhope.

OSBORNE *and* RALEIGH *come down the steps.*

Well, Osborne. Everything ready?

OSBORNE: Yes, I think we're all ready, sir. I make it just a quarter to.

COLONEL: That's right.

OSBORNE: The men are going to stand by at three minutes to.

COLONEL: The smoke bombs drop exactly on the hour. You'll give the word to go when the smoke's thick enough?

OSBORNE: That's right, sir.

STANHOPE (*at the servant's dug-out*): Mason!

MASON: Coming, sir!

STANHOPE: Were the men having their rum, Uncle?

OSBORNE: Yes. Just as we left. It gives it a quarter of an hour to soak in.

COLONEL: That's right. Are they cheerful?

OSBORNE: Yes. Quite.

MASON *brings in two cups of coffee and puts them on table.*

STANHOPE: Would you like to go up and speak to them, sir?

COLONEL: Well, don't you think they'd rather be left alone?

STANHOPE: I think they would appreciate a word or two.

COLONEL: All right. If you think they would.

OSBORNE: They're all in the centre dug-out, sir.

COLONEL: Right. You coming, Stanhope?

STANHOPE: Yes. I'll come, sir.

The COLONEL *lingers a moment. There is an awkward pause. Then the* COLONEL *clears his throat and speaks.*

COLONEL: Well, good luck, Osborne. I'm certain you'll put up a good show.

OSBORNE (*taking the* COLONEL's *hand*): Thank you, sir.

COLONEL: And, Raleigh, just go in like blazes. Grab hold of the first Boche you see and bundle him across here. One'll do, but bring more if you see any handy.

RALEIGH (*taking the* COLONEL's *offered hand*): Right, sir.

COLONEL: And, if you succeed, I'll recommend you both for the M.C.

OSBORNE *and* RALEIGH *murmur their thanks.*

Remember, a great deal may depend on bringing in a German. It may mean the winning of the whole war. You never know. (*Another pause.*) Well, good luck to you both.

Again OSBORNE *and* RALEIGH *murmur their thanks. The* COLONEL *and* STANHOPE *go towards the door.*

(*Over his shoulder.*) Don't forget to empty your pockets of papers and things.

RALEIGH: Oh, no. (*He goes into his dug-out, taking letters and papers from his pockets.*)

STANHOPE *is about to follow the* COLONEL *up the steps when* OSBORNE *calls him back.*

OSBORNE: Er—Stanhope—just a moment.

STANHOPE (*returning*): Hullo!

OSBORNE: I say, don't think I'm being morbid, or anything like that, but would you mind taking these?

STANHOPE: Sure. Until you come back, old man.

OSBORNE: It's only just in case—— (*He takes a letter and his watch from his tunic pocket and puts it on the table. Then he pulls off his ring.*) If anything should happen, would you send these along to my wife? (*He pauses, and gives an awkward little laugh.*)

STANHOPE (*putting the articles together on the table*): You're coming back, old man. Damn it! what on earth should I do without you?

OSBORNE (*laughing*): Goodness knows!

STANHOPE: Must have somebody to tuck me up in bed. (*There is a pause.*) Well, I'll see you up in the sap, before you go. Just have a spot of rum in that coffee.

OSBORNE: Righto.

STANHOPE *goes to the steps and lingers for a moment.*

STANHOPE: Cheero!

For a second their eyes meet; they laugh. STANHOPE *goes slowly up the steps.*

There is silence in the dug-out. OSBORNE *has been filling his pipe, and stands lighting it as* RALEIGH *returns.*

OSBORNE: Just time for a small pipe.

RALEIGH: Good. I'll have a cigarette, I think. (*He feels in his pocket.*)

OSBORNE: Here you are. (*He offers his case to* RALEIGH.)

RALEIGH: I say, I'm always smoking yours.

OSBORNE: That's all right. (*Pause.*) What about this coffee?

RALEIGH: Sure.

They sit at the table.

OSBORNE: Are you going to have a drop of rum in it?

RALEIGH: Don't you think it might make us a—a bit muzzy?

OSBORNE: I'm just having the coffee as it is.

RALEIGH: I think I will, too.

OSBORNE: We'll have the rum afterwards—to celebrate.

RALEIGH: That's a much better idea.

They stir their coffee in silence. OSBORNE'S *eyes meet* RALEIGH'S. *He smiles.*

OSBORNE: How d'you feel?

RALEIGH: All right.

OSBORNE: I've got a sort of empty feeling inside.

RALEIGH: That's just what I've got!

OSBORNE: Wind up!

RALEIGH: I keep wanting to yawn.

OSBORNE: That's it. Wind up. I keep wanting to yawn too. It'll pass off directly we start.

RALEIGH (*taking a deep breath*): I wish we could go now.

OSBORNE (*looking at his watch on the table*): We've got eight minutes yet.

RALEIGH: Oh, Lord!

OSBORNE: Let's just have a last look at the map. (*He picks up the map and spreads it out.*) Directly the smoke's thick enough, I'll give the word. You run straight for this point here——

RALEIGH: When I get to the Boche wire I lie down and wait for you.

OSBORNE: Don't forget to throw your bombs.

RALEIGH (*patting his pocket*): No. I've got them here.

OSBORNE: When I shout " Righto! "—in you go with your eight men. I shall lie on the Boche parapet, and blow my whistle now and then to show you where I am. Pounce on the first Boche you see and bundle him out to me.

RALEIGH: Righto.

OSBORNE: Then we come back like blazes.

RALEIGH: The whole thing'll be over quite quickly?

OSBORNE: I reckon with luck we shall be back in three minutes.

RALEIGH: As quick as that?

OSBORNE: I think so. (*He folds up the map.*) And now let's forget all about it for—(*he looks at his watch*)—for six minutes

RALEIGH: Oh, Lord, I can't!

OSBORNE: You must.

RALEIGH: How topping if we both get the M.C.!

OSBORNE: Yes. (*Pause.*) Your coffee sweet enough?

RALEIGH: Yes, thanks. It's jolly good coffee. (*Pause.*) I wonder what the Boche are doing over there now?

OSBORNE: I don't know. D'you like coffee better than tea?

RALEIGH: I do for breakfast. (*Pause.*) Do these smoke bombs make much row when they burst?

OSBORNE: Not much. (*Pause.*) Personally, I like cocoa for breakfast.

RALEIGH (*laughing*): I'm sorry!

OSBORNE: Why sorry? Why shouldn't I have cocoa for breakfast?

RALEIGH: I don't mean that. I—mean—I'm sorry to keep talking about the raid. It's so difficult to—to talk about anything else. I was just wondering—will the Boche retaliate in any way after the raid?

OSBORNE: Bound to—a bit.

RALEIGH: Shelling?

OSBORNE:

"'The time has come,' the Walrus said,
'To talk of many things:
Of shoes—and ships—and sealing wax—
Of cabbages—and kings.'"

RALEIGH:

"'And why the sea is boiling hot—
And whether pigs have wings.'"

OSBORNE: Now we're off! Quick, let's talk about pigs! Black pigs or white pigs?

RALEIGH: Black pigs. In the New Forest you find them, quite wild.

OSBORNE: You know the New Forest?

RALEIGH: Rather! My home's down there. A little place called Allum Green, just outside Lyndhurst.

OSBORNE: I know Lyndhurst well.

RALEIGH: It's rather nice down there.

OSBORNE: I like it more than any place I know.

RALEIGH: I think I do, too. Of course, it's different when you've always lived in a place.

OSBORNE: You like it in a different way.

RALEIGH: Yes. Just behind our house there's a stream called the Highland; it runs for miles—right through the middle of the forest. Dennis and I followed it once as far as we could.

OSBORNE: I used to walk a lot round Lyndhurst.

RALEIGH: I wish we'd known each other then. You could have come with Dennis and me.

OSBORNE: I wish I had. I used to walk alone.

RALEIGH: You must come and stay with us one day.

OSBORNE: I should like to—awfully.

RALEIGH: I can show you places in the forest that nobody knows about except Dennis and me. It gets thicker and darker and cooler, and you stir up all kinds of funny wild animals.

OSBORNE: They say there are ruins, somewhere in the forest, of villages that William the Conqueror pulled down to let the forest grow.

RALEIGH: I know. We often used to look for them, but we haven't found them yet. (*Pause.*) You must come and help look one day.

OSBORNE: I'll find them all right.

RALEIGH: Then you can write to the papers. " Dramatic Discovery of Professor Osborne ! "

OSBORNE *laughs.*

OSBORNE: I did go exploring once—digging up Roman remains.

RALEIGH: Where was that?

OSBORNE: Near my home in Sussex there's a Roman road called Stane Street; it runs as straight as a line from the coast to London.

RALEIGH: I know it.

OSBORNE: Near where I live the road runs over Bignor Hill, but in recent times a new road's been cut round the foot of the hill, meeting the old road again farther on. The old road over the hill hasn't been used for years and years—and it's all grown over with grass, and bushes and trees grow in the middle of it.

RALEIGH: Can you still see where it runs?

OSBORNE: Quite easily, in places.

RALEIGH: Did you dig a bit of it up, then?

OSBORNE: Yes. We got permission to dig out a section. It was in wonderful condition.

RALEIGH: Did you find anything?

OSBORNE: We found a horseshoe—and a Roman penny.

RALEIGH (*laughing*): Splendid!

OSBORNE: It's awfully fascinating, digging like that.

RALEIGH: It must be.

OSBORNE *glances at his watch.*

Is it time yet?

OSBORNE: Two minutes. Then we must go up. I wish we had a good hot bath waiting for us when we get back.

RALEIGH: So do I. (*Pause.*) We're having something special for dinner, aren't we?

OSBORNE: How did you know? It's supposed to be a secret.

RALEIGH: Mason dropped a hint.

OSBORNE: Well, we've had a fresh chicken sent up from Noyelle Farm.

RALEIGH: I say!

OSBORNE: And a most awful luxury—two bottles of champagne and half a dozen cigars! One each, and one spare one in case one explodes.

RALEIGH: I've never smoked a cigar.

OSBORNE: It's bound to make you sick.

RALEIGH *notices* OSBORNE'S *ring on the table; he picks it up.*

RALEIGH: I say, here's your ring.

OSBORNE: Yes. I'm—I'm leaving it here. I don't want the risk of losing it.

RALEIGH: Oh! (*There is silence. He puts the ring slowly down.*)

OSBORNE (*rising*): Well, I think perhaps we ought to get ready.

RALEIGH: Yes. Righto. (*He also rises.*)

OSBORNE: I'm not going to wear a belt—just my revolver, with the lanyard round my neck.

RALEIGH: I see. (*He puts his lanyard round his neck and grips his revolver.*) I feel better with this in my hand, don't you?

OSBORNE: Yes. Something to hold. Loaded all right?

RALEIGH: Yes.

They put on their helmets. OSBORNE takes his pipe from his mouth and lays it carefully on the table.

OSBORNE: I do hate leaving a pipe when it's got a nice glow on the top like that.

RALEIGH (*with a short laugh*): What a pity!

There is another pause. OSBORNE glances at his watch as it lies on the table.

OSBORNE: Three minutes to. I think we'd better go.

RALEIGH: Righto.

Their eyes meet as OSBORNE turns from the table.

OSBORNE: I'm glad it's you and I—together, Raleigh.

RALEIGH (*eagerly*): Are you—really?

OSBORNE: Yes.

RALEIGH: So am I—awfully.

OSBORNE: We must put up a good show.

RALEIGH: Yes. Rather!

There is a short pause.

OSBORNE: Let's go along, shall we?

RALEIGH: Righto.

They go towards the steps.

MASON *comes to the entrance of his dug-out as they pass.*

MASON: Good luck, sir.

OSBORNE: Thanks, Mason.

MASON: Good luck, Mr. Raleigh.

RALEIGH: Thanks.

OSBORNE *and* RALEIGH *go up together into the pale evening sun.*

MASON *tidies the papers on the table; picks up the two coffee mugs, and goes away.*

There is silence in the trenches above the deserted dug-out. Then, suddenly, there comes the dull " crush " of bursting smoke bombs, followed in a second by the vicious rattle of machine-guns. The red and green glow of German alarm rockets comes faintly through the dug-out door. Then comes the thin whistle and crash of falling shells; first one by itself, then two, almost together. Quicker and quicker they come, till the noise mingles together in confused turmoil. Yet the noise is deadened by the earth walls of the tiny dug-out, and comes quite softly till the whine of one shell rises above the others to a shriek and a crash. A dark funnel of earth leaps up beyond the parapet of the trench outside; earth falls and rattles down the steps, and a black cloud of smoke rises slowly out of sight. Gradually the noise dies away—there is a longer pause between the crash of each bursting shell. The machine-guns stop—rattle again and stop—rattle for the last time—and stop.

Voices are calling in the trench outside; STANHOPE'S *voice is heard:*

STANHOPE: All right, sir. Come down quickly!

COLONEL: How many?

STANHOPE: Only one.

Another shell whines and shrieks and crashes near by. There is silence for a moment, then STANHOPE *speaks again.*

Hurt, sir?

COLONEL: No. It's all right.

STANHOPE, *pale and haggard, comes down the steps, followed by the* COLONEL.

STANHOPE (*calling up the steps*): Bring him down, sergeant-major.

S.-M. (*above*): Coming, sir.

STANHOPE (*to the* COLONEL): You won't want me, will you?

COLONEL: Well—er——

STANHOPE: I want to go and see those men.

COLONEL: Oh, all right.

STANHOPE goes to the door, making way for the SERGEANT-MAJOR *to come down, followed by a bareheaded* GERMAN BOY, *in field grey, sobbing bitterly. Behind come two* SOLDIERS *with fixed bayonets.*

STANHOPE goes up the steps.

The SERGEANT-MAJOR *takes the* GERMAN BOY *by the arm and draws him into the centre of the dug-out to face the* COLONEL, *who has seated himself at the table. The two* SOLDIERS *stand behind.*

S.-M. (*soothingly to the* GERMAN BOY): All right, sonny, we ain't going to 'urt you.

Suddenly the BOY *falls on his knees and sobs out some words in broken English.*

GERMAN: Mercy—mister—mercy!

S.-M.: Come on, lad, get up. (*With a huge fist he takes the* BOY *by the collar and draws him to his feet.*)

The BOY *sobs hysterically.*

The COLONEL *clears his throat and begins in somewhat poor German.*

COLONEL: Was ist sein Regiment?

GERMAN: Wurtembergisches.

COLONEL: Was ist der nummer von sein Regiment?

GERMAN: Zwanzig.

COLONEL (*making a note*): Twentieth Wurtembergers. (*He looks up again.*) Wann kommen sie hier?

GERMAN: Gestern abend.

COLONEL (*making a note and looking up again*): Wo kommen sie hier?

GERMAN (*after a moment's thought*): Mein Geburtsort?

COLONEL (*forgetting himself for a moment*): What's that?

GERMAN (*in halting English*): You—wish—to know—where I was—born?

COLONEL: No! What town did you come up to the line from?

GERMAN (*after a little hesitation*): I—do not tell you.

COLONEL: Oh, well, that's all right. (*To the* SERGEANT-MAJOR) Search him.

The SERGEANT-MAJOR'S *big fists grope over the* BOY'S *pockets. He produces a small book.*

S.-M. (*giving it to the* COLONEL): Looks like 'is pay-book, sir.

COLONEL (*looking eagerly into the book*): Good.

The SERGEANT-MAJOR *has found a pocket-book; the* GERMAN BOY *clutches at it impulsively.*

S.-M.: 'Ere, stop that!

GERMAN: Lassen sie mich! (*He pauses.*) Let—me—please—keep —that.

S.-M. (*very embarrassed*): You let go! (*He wrenches the case away and gives it to the* COLONEL.)

COLONEL (*glancing at the papers in the case*): Look like letters. May be useful. Is that all, sergeant-major?

S.-M. (*looking at a few articles in his hands*): 'Ere's a few oddments, sir—bit o' string, sir; little box o' fruit drops; pocket-knife, sir; bit o' cedar pencil—and a stick o' chocolate, sir.

COLONEL: Let him have those back, except the pocket-knife.

S.-M.: Very good, sir. (*He turns to the* GERMAN BOY *with a smile.*) 'Ere you are, sonny.

The GERMAN BOY *takes back the oddments.*

COLONEL: All right, sergeant-major. Send him straight back to my headquarters. I'll question him again there.

S.-M.: Very good, sir. (*He turns to the* GERMAN.) Come on, sonny, up you go. (*He points up the steps.*)

The GERMAN BOY, *calm now, bows stiffly to the* COLONEL *and goes away, followed by the two* SOLDIERS *and the* SERGEANT-MAJOR.

The COLONEL *is deeply absorbed in the German's pay-book. He mutters "Splendid!" to himself, then looks at his watch and rises quickly.*

STANHOPE *comes slowly down the steps.*

COLONEL (*excitedly*): Splendid, Stanhope! We've got all we wanted—20th Wurtembergers! His regiment came into the line last night. I must go right away and 'phone the brigadier. He'll be very pleased about it. It's a feather in our cap, Stanhope.

STANHOPE has given one look of astonishment at the COLONEL and strolled past him. He turns at the table and speaks in a dead voice.

STANHOPE: How awfully nice—if the brigadier's pleased.

The COLONEL stares at STANHOPE and suddenly collects himself.

COLONEL: Oh—er—what about the raiding-party—are they all safely back.

STANHOPE: Did you expect them to be all safely back, sir?

COLONEL: Oh—er—what—er——

STANHOPE: Four men and Raleigh came safely back, sir.

COLONEL: Oh, I say, I'm sorry! That's—er—six men and—er—Osborne?

STANHOPE: Yes, sir.

COLONEL: I'm very sorry. Poor Osborne!

STANHOPE: Still it'll be awfully nice if the brigadier's pleased.

COLONEL: Don't be silly, Stanhope. Do you know—er—what happened to Osborne?

STANHOPE: A hand grenade—while he was waiting for Raleigh.

COLONEL: I'm very sorry. And the six men?

STANHOPE: Machine-gun bullets, I suppose.

COLONEL: Yes. I was afraid—er——

His words trail away; he fidgets uneasily as STANHOPE looks at him with a pale, expressionless face.

RALEIGH comes slowly down the steps, walking as though he were asleep; his hands are bleeding.

The COLONEL turns to the boy with enthusiasm.

Very well done, Raleigh. Well done, my boy. I'll get you a Military Cross for this! Splendid!

RALEIGH looks at the COLONEL and tries to speak. He raises his hand to his forehead and sways. The COLONEL takes him by the arm.

Sit down here, my boy.

RALEIGH *sits on the edge of* OSBORNE'S *bed.*

Have a good rest. Well, I must be off. (*He moves towards the steps, and, turning once more to* RALEIGH *as he leaves*) Very well done. (*With a quick glance at* STANHOPE, *the* COLONEL *goes away.*)

There is silence now in the trenches outside; the last shell has whistled over and crashed. Dusk is beginning to fall over the German lines. The glow of Very lights begins to rise and fade against the evening sky. STANHOPE *is staring dumbly at the table—at* OSBORNE'S *watch and ring. Presently he turns his haggard face towards* RALEIGH, *who sits with lowered head, looking at the palms of his hands.*

STANHOPE *moves slowly across towards the doorway, and pauses to look down at* RALEIGH. RALEIGH *looks up into* STANHOPE'S *face, and their eyes meet. When* STANHOPE *speaks, his voice is still expressionless and dead.*

STANHOPE: Must you sit on Osborne's bed?

He turns and goes slowly up the steps.

RALEIGH *rises unsteadily, murmurs* " Sorry " *and stands with lowered head.*

Heavy guns are booming miles away.

THE CURTAIN FALLS

SCENE 2

Late evening on the same day.

The dug-out is lit quite festively by an unusual number of candles. Two champagne bottles stand prominent on the table. Dinner is over.

STANHOPE, *with a cigar between his teeth, lounges across the table, one elbow among the plates and mugs. His hair is ruffled; there is a bright red flush on his cheeks. He has just made a remark which has sent* HIBBERT *and* TROTTER *into uproarious laughter; he listens with a smile.* TROTTER *is sitting on the box to the right of the table, leaning back against the wall. A cigar is embedded in his podgy fingers; his face is a shiny scarlet, with deep red patches below the ears. The three bottom buttons of his tunic are undone, and now and then his hand steals gently over his distended stomach.* HIBBERT *sits on the bed to the left, his thin white fingers nervously twitching the ash from his cigar. His pale face is shiny with sweat from the heat of the candles; his laugh is high-pitched and excited.* TROTTER *speaks in a husky voice as the laughter dies away.*

TROTTER: And what did she say to that?

STANHOPE: She said, " Not in these trousers "—in French.

TROTTER *and* HIBBERT *burst into laughter again.*

TROTTER (*coughing and wheezing*): Oh—dear-o-dear!

STANHOPE: I simply drew myself up and said, " Very well, mam'sel, have it your own way."

TROTTER: And she did?

STANHOPE: No.   She didn't.

Again the others laugh. TROTTER *wipes a tear from his eye.*

TROTTER: Oh, skipper, you *are* a scream—and no mistake!

HIBBERT: I never forget picking up a couple of tarts one night and taking 'em out to dinner.

TROTTER (*winking at* STANHOPE): 'E's orf again.

HIBBERT: We drank enough bubbly to sink a battleship——

STANHOPE: To *float* a battleship.

HIBBERT: Well—to float a battleship. Then I took 'em for a joy-ride out to Maidenhead—did sixty all the way. We danced a bit at Skindles, and drank a lot of port and muck. Then damned if I didn't lose the way coming back—got landed miles from anywhere. And those tarts began cursing me like hell—said I'd done it on purpose. I said if they didn't damn well shut up I'd chuck 'em both out in the road and leave 'em.

STANHOPE (*ironically*): Hurrah!   That's the idea!   Treat 'em rough!

HIBBERT (*giggling*): That shut 'em up all right! Then I started doing about sixty down all sorts of roads—I went round a corner on two wheels with those girls' hair on end—didn't have any more trouble from *them*! (*He chuckles at the memory, and takes an unsteady gulp of champagne.*)

STANHOPE: You're the sort of man who makes girls hard to please.

TROTTER (*heavily*): Well, I never 'ad no motor-car; my old lady and me used to walk; legs is good enough for me.

STANHOPE: You satisfied with legs?

TROTTER: *I* am—yes!

STANHOPE: Much cheaper.

HIBBERT (*laughing delightedly*): That's damn good!

STANHOPE (*raising his mug*): Well, here's a toast to legs—God bless 'em!

HIBBERT (*raising his mug*): Good old legs!

TROTTER (*raising his mug*): Shanks' mare.

STANHOPE: Shanks' *what*?

TROTTER: Shanks' mare, they call 'em.

STANHOPE: Call what?

TROTTER: Why—legs.

HIBBERT (*almost screaming with delight*): Oh, Trotter! you're a dream!

TROTTER (*turning a baleful eye on* HIBBERT): You've 'ad too much champagne, you 'ave.

HIBBERT *takes a leather case from his pocket and produces some picture post-cards.*

HIBBERT: I say, I've never shown you these, have I?

He hands them one by one to STANHOPE, *smiling up into* STAN-HOPE's *face for approval.*

STANHOPE: Where did you get these from?

HIBBERT: In Bethune. (*He hands up a card.*) *She's* all right, isn't she?

STANHOPE: Too fat.

HIBBERT (*looking over* STANHOPE's *shoulder*): Oh, I don't know.

STANHOPE: Much too fat. (*He hands the card to* TROTTER.) What do you think, Trotter?

TROTTER *takes a pair of pince-nez from his pocket, balances them on his fat nose, and looks at the picture.*

HIBBERT: All right, isn't she?

TROTTER: Well, I don't know. If you ask me, I'd rather 'ave a decent picture of Margate Pier.

HIBBERT (*impatiently*): Oh, you don't understand *art*. (*He hands another card to* STANHOPE.) There's a nice pair of legs for you.

STANHOPE: Too thin—aren't they, Trotter? (*He hands* TROTTER *the card.*)

TROTTER (*after some thought*): Scraggy, I call 'em.

HIBBERT (*handing* STANHOPE *another card*): *That's* the one I like best.

STANHOPE: Not bad.

HIBBERT: Glorious bedroom eyes.

STANHOPE: She's all right.

HIBBERT: Ever see that show *Zip* at the Hippodrome? Couple of damn fine girls in that—twins. Did you see 'em, skipper?

STANHOPE (*wearily*): I don't know—seen stacks of shows—can't remember them all. (*He brightens up.*) Now then, swallow up that bubbly! Hi! Mason!

MASON: Yessir!

MASON *appears.*

STANHOPE: Bring some whisky.

MASON: Yessir.

He disappears.

TROTTER: What? Whisky on top of champagne?

STANHOPE: Why not? It's all right.

TROTTER: Well, I don't know; doesn't sound right to me. I feel as if somebody's blown me up with a bicycle pump.

STANHOPE: You look it, too.

TROTTER (*blowing a stream of cigar smoke up to the dark ceiling:*) Any'ow, it was a jolly fine bit o' chicken—and I'd go a mile any day for a chunk o' that jam pudding.

MASON *brings a bottle of whisky.*

STANHOPE: Your pudding's made Mr. Trotter feel all blown out, Mason.

MASON: I'm sorry, sir; it wasn't meant, sir.

TROTTER: It was all right, Mason, take it from me. I know a decent bit o' pudden when I see it.

MASON: It was only boiled ration biscuits and jam, sir. (*He turns to* STANHOPE.) I thought I better tell you, sir—this is the last bottle.

STANHOPE: The last bottle! Why, damn it, we brought six!

MASON: I know, sir. But five's gone.

STANHOPE: Where the devil's it gone to?

MASON: Well, sir, you remember there was one on the first night—and then one——

STANHOPE: Oh, for Lord's sake, don't go through them one by one; this'll last till sunrise. (*He turns to* TROTTER *and* HIBBERT) Sunrise tomorrow, my lads!

TROTTER: Oh, forget that.

STANHOPE: You bet we will! Now then! Who's for a spot of whisky?

TROTTER: I reckon I'm about full up. I'd like a nice cup o' tea, Mason.

MASON: Very good, sir.

He goes out.

STANHOPE: Tea!

TROTTER: Yes. That's what I want. Decent cup o' tea. Still, I'll just 'ave about a spoonful o' whisky—got a touch of palpitations.

STANHOPE: Here you are—say when!

TROTTER: Wo! That's enough!

STANHOPE: You'll have a decent spot, won't you, Hibbert?

HIBBERT: Yes. I'm game!

TROTTER (*stifling a hiccup*): Just a cup o' tea—then I'll go and relieve young Raleigh. Pity 'e didn't come down to supper.

STANHOPE: I told him to. I told him to come down for an hour and let the sergeant-major take over.

TROTTER: I wonder why 'e didn't come.

HIBBERT: That lad's too keen on his " duty." He told me he liked being up there with the men better than down here with us.

STANHOPE (*quietly*): He *said* that?

HIBBERT: Yes. I told him about the chicken and champagne and cigars—and he stared at me and said, " You're not having that, are you? "—just as if he thought we were going to chuck it away!

TROTTER: I reckon that raid shook 'im up more'n we thought. I like that youngster. 'E's got pluck. Strong lad, too—the way he came back through the smoke after that raid, carrying that Boche under 'is arm like a baby.

HIBBERT: Did you see him afterwards, though? He came into that dug-out and never said a word—didn't seem to know where he was.

TROTTER: Well, 'e's only a lad.

STANHOPE (*to* HIBBERT): He actually told you he preferred being up with the men better than down here?

HIBBERT: That's what he said.

TROTTER: Well, I 'ope 'e gets the M.C., that's all; 'e's just the kid I'd like if ever I 'ave a kid—strong and plucky.

STANHOPE: Oh, for God's sake forget that bloody raid! Think I want to talk about it?

TROTTER (*surprised*): No—but, after all——

STANHOPE: Well—shut up!

TROTTER (*uneasily*): All right—all right.

STANHOPE: We were having a jolly decent evening till you started blabbing about the war.

TROTTER: *I* didn't start it.

STANHOPE: You did.

TROTTER: You began it about——

STANHOPE: Well, for God's sake stop it, then!

TROTTER: All right—all right.

HIBBERT: Did I ever tell you the story about the girl I met in Soho?

STANHOPE: I don't know—I expect you did.

HIBBERT (*undismayed*): It'll amuse you. I'd been to a dance, and I was coming home quite late——

STANHOPE: Yes, and it's late now. You go on duty at eleven. You better go and get some sleep.

HIBBERT: It's all right. I'm as fresh as a daisy.

STANHOPE: You may be. But go to bed.

HIBBERT: What?

STANHOPE (*louder*): I said, " Go to bed! "

HIBBERT: I say, that's a nice end to a jolly evening!

STANHOPE: I'm sorry. I'm tired.

HIBBERT (*perkily*): Well, *you* better go to bed!

There is silence. STANHOPE *looks at* HIBBERT, *who sniggers.*

STANHOPE: What was that you said?

HIBBERT: I was only joking.

STANHOPE: I asked you what you said.

HIBBERT: I said, " *You* better go to bed."

STANHOPE's *flushed face is looking full into* HIBBERT's. HIBBERT *gives the ghost of a snigger.*

STANHOPE: Clear out of here!

HIBBERT (*rising unsteadily*): What—what d'you mean.

STANHOPE: Get out of here, for God's sake!

HIBBERT (*blustering*): I say—look here——

STANHOPE: Get out of my sight!

With a frightened glance at STANHOPE, HIBBERT *sneaks quietly away into his dug-out.*

There is silence, and the guns can be heard—deep and ominous.

Little worm gets on my nerves.

TROTTER: Poor little bloke. Never seen 'im so cheerful before out 'ere.

STANHOPE: Doesn't he nearly drive you mad?

TROTTER: I reckon 'e only wanted to keep cheerful.

STANHOPE: Doesn't his repulsive little mind make you *sick*?

MASON brings TROTTER'S *mug of tea and goes away.*

I envy you, Trotter. Nothing upsets you, does it? You're always the same.

TROTTER: Always the same, am I? (*He sighs.*) Little you know——

STANHOPE: You never get sick to death of everything, or so happy you want to sing.

TROTTER: I don't know—I whistle sometimes.

STANHOPE: But you always *feel* the same.

TROTTER: I feel all blown out now.

There is a pause. TROTTER *sips his tea and* STANHOPE *takes a whisky.*

'Ere's 'Ibbert's post-cards. Funny a bloke carrying pictures like this about. Satisfies 'is lust, I s'pose—poor little feller. (*He rises.*) Well, I'll go and relieve young Raleigh. Pity 'e didn't come down to supper. (*He tries to button his tunic, without success. He buckles his webbing belt over his unbuttoned tunic, puts on his helmet, and slings his respirator over his shoulder.*) Well, cheero!

STANHOPE: You realise you're my second-in-command now, don't you?

TROTTER: Well, you 'adn't said nothing about it, but——

STANHOPE: Well, you are.

TROTTER: Righto, skipper. (*He pauses.*) Thanks. (*He goes towards the door.*) I won't let you down.

STANHOPE: After your duty, have a decent sleep. We must be ready at half-past five.

TROTTER: Righto, skipper. Well, I'll be going up. Give me a chance to cool off up there. It's as 'ot as 'ell in 'ere, with all them damn candles burning.

STANHOPE: I suppose it is. My head's nearly splitting. (*He blows out three of the candles, leaving the dim light of one.*)

TROTTER (*half up the steps*): There's a bit of a mist rising.

STANHOPE (*dully*): Is there?

> TROTTER *disappears into the night.*

> STANHOPE *broods over the table.*

> Mason!

MASON (*outside*): Yessir!

STANHOPE: You can bring Mr. Raleigh's dinner.

MASON: Very good, sir.

> MASON *brings a plate of steaming food, gathering up and taking away some of the used crockery. Presently* RALEIGH *comes slowly down the steps. He pauses at the bottom, takes off his helmet, and hesitates.*

> STANHOPE *is sitting at the table puffing at the remains of his cigar. There is silence except for the rumble of the guns.*

STANHOPE: I thought I told you to come down to dinner at eight o'clock?

RALEIGH: Oh, I'm sorry. I didn't think you—er——

STANHOPE: Well? You didn't think I—er—what?

RALEIGH: I didn't think you'd—you'd mind—if I didn't.

STANHOPE: I see. And why do you think I asked you—if I didn't mind?

RALEIGH: I'm sorry.

STANHOPE: Well, we've kept your dinner. It's ready for you here.

RALEIGH: Oh, it's awfully good of you to have kept it for me, but—I—I had something to eat up there.

STANHOPE: You—had something to eat up there? What do you mean, exactly?

RALEIGH: They brought the tea round while I was on duty. I had a cup, and some bread and cheese.

STANHOPE: Are you telling me—you've been feeding with the men?

RALEIGH: Well, Sergeant Baker suggested——

STANHOPE: So you take your orders from Sergeant Baker, do you?

RALEIGH: No, but——

STANHOPE: You eat the men's rations when there's barely enough for each man?

RALEIGH: They asked me to share.

STANHOPE: Now, look here. I know you're new to this, but I thought you'd have the common sense to leave the men alone to their meals. Do you think they want an officer prowling round eating their rations, and sucking up to them like that? My officers are here to be respected—not laughed at.

RALEIGH: Why did they ask me—if they didn't mean it?

STANHOPE: Don't you realise they were making a fool of you?

RALEIGH: Why should they?

STANHOPE: So you know more about my men than I do?

There is silence. RALEIGH *is facing* STANHOPE *squarely.*

RALEIGH: I'm sorry then—if I was wrong.

STANHOPE: Sit down.

RALEIGH: It's all right, thanks.

STANHOPE (*suddenly shouting*): *Sit down!*

RALEIGH *sits on the box to the right of the table.* STANHOPE *speaks quietly again.*

I understand you prefer being up there with the men than down here with us?

RALEIGH: I don't see what you mean.

STANHOPE: What did you tell Hibbert?

RALEIGH: Hibbert? I—I didn't say——

STANHOPE: Don't lie.

RALEIGH (*rising*): I'm not lying! Why should I—lie?

STANHOPE: Then why didn't you come down to supper when I told you to?

RALEIGH: I—I wasn't hungry. I had rather a headache. It's cooler up there.

STANHOPE: You insulted Trotter and Hibbert by not coming. You realise that, I suppose?

RALEIGH: I didn't mean to do anything like that.

STANHOPE: Well, you did. You know now—don't you?

RALEIGH makes no reply. He is trying to understand why STAN-HOPE'S temper has risen to a trembling fury. STANHOPE can scarcely control his voice.

(*Loudly.*) I say—you *know* now, don't you?

RALEIGH: Yes, I'm sorry.

STANHOPE: My officers work *together*. I'll have no damn prigs.

RALEIGH: I'll speak to Trotter and Hibbert. I didn't realise——

STANHOPE raises his cigar. His hand trembles so violently that he can scarcely take the cigar between his teeth. RALEIGH looks at STANHOPE, fascinated and horrified.

STANHOPE: What are you looking at?

RALEIGH (*lowering his head*): Nothing.

STANHOPE: Anything—*funny* about me?

RALEIGH: No.

After a moment's silence, RALEIGH speaks in a low, halting voice.
I'm awfully sorry, Dennis, if—if I annoyed you by coming to your company.

STANHOPE: What on *earth* are you talking about? What do you mean?

RALEIGH: You resent my being here.

STANHOPE: Resent you *being* here?

RALEIGH: Ever since I came——

STANHOPE: I don't know what you mean. I resent you being a damn fool, that's all. (*There is a pause.*) Better eat your dinner before it's cold.

RALEIGH: I'm not hungry, thanks.

STANHOPE: Oh, for God's sake, sit down and eat it like a man!

RALEIGH: I can't eat it, thanks.

STANHOPE (*shouting*): Are you going to eat your dinner?

RALEIGH: Good God! Don't you understand? How *can* I sit down and eat that—when—(*his voice is nearly breaking*)—when Osborne's—lying—out there——

STANHOPE rises slowly. His eyes are wide and staring; he is fighting for breath, and his words come brokenly.

STANHOPE: My God! You bloody little swine! You think I don't care—you think you're the only soul that cares!

RALEIGH: And yet you can sit there and drink champagne—and smoke cigars——

STANHOPE: The one man I could trust—my best friend—the one man I could talk to as man to man—who understood everything—and you think I don't care——

RALEIGH: But how can you when——?

STANHOPE: To forget, you little fool—to forget! D'you understand? To forget! You think there's no limit to what a man can bear?

He turns quickly from RALEIGH and goes to the dark corner by OSBORNE'S bed. He stands with his face towards the wall, his shoulders heaving as he fights for breath.

RALEIGH: I'm awfully sorry, Dennis. I—I didn't understand.

STANHOPE makes no reply.

You don't know how—I——

STANHOPE: Go away, please—leave me alone.

RALEIGH: Can't I-——

STANHOPE turns wildly upon RALEIGH.

STANHOPE: Oh, get out! For God's sake, get out!

RALEIGH goes away into his dug-out, and STANHOPE is alone. The Very lights rise and fall outside, softly breaking the darkness with their glow—sometimes steel-blue, sometimes grey. Through the night there comes the impatient grumble of gunfire that never dies away.

THE CURTAIN FALLS

Towards dawn. The candles are no longer burning. The intense darkness of the dug-out is softened by the glow of the Very lights in the sky beyond the doorway. There is no sound except the distant mutter of the guns.

A man comes from the servant's dug-out; for a moment his head and shoulders stand out black against the glowing sky, then he passes on into the darkness by the table. There comes the rasp of a striking match—a tiny flame—and a candle gleams. MASON blinks in the light and turns to STANHOPE's bed. STANHOPE lies huddled with his blanket drawn tightly round him.

MASON (*softly*): Sir——

STANHOPE *does not move;* MASON *shakes him gently by the knee.*

(*A little louder.*) Sir——

STANHOPE: Yes? (*There is a pause.*) That you, Mason?

MASON: 'Arf-past five, sir.

STANHOPE: Oh, right. (*He raises himself on his elbow.*) I was only half asleep. I keep on waking up. It's so frightfully cold in here.

MASON: It's a cold dug-out, this one, sir. I've made some 'ot tea.

STANHOPE: Good. You might bring me some.

MASON: Right you are, sir.

STANHOPE: And take some to the officers in there—and wake them up.

MASON: Very good, sir.

MASON *goes to his dug-out.*

STANHOPE *rises stiffly from his bed, shudders from the cold, and slowly begins putting his equipment on.*

TROTTER *wanders in from his dug-out vigorously lathering his face. He is dressed, except for his collar.*

TROTTER: Wash and brush-up, tuppence!

STANHOPE (*looking up, surprised*): Hullo! I thought you were asleep.

TROTTER: I 'ad a decent sleep when I come off dooty. What's the time?

STANHOPE: Half-past five. It'll be getting light soon. You better buck up.

TROTTER: All right. *I* shan't be long. Sounds quiet enough out there.

STANHOPE: Yes.

MASON *brings four mugs of tea.*

TROTTER: Ah! that's what I want. A decent cup of tea.

MASON (*putting a mug on the table for* STANHOPE): Nice and 'ot, sir. I've cut a packet of sambridges for each gentleman, sir.

STANHOPE: Good.

MASON *takes the other mugs of tea into the right-hand dug-out.* TROTTER *follows, lathering with gusto.*

STANHOPE: You might give Hibbert and Raleigh a call.

TROTTER: I woke 'em up, skipper. They're getting their things on.

MASON *returns.*

STANHOPE: When you've cleared up your kitchen, you must dress and join your platoon in the line.

MASON: Very good, sir.

STANHOPE: If things are going well at eleven o'clock, come down here and do your best to get some lunch for us. We shall come down in turn as we can.

MASON: Very good, sir.

STANHOPE *sits at the table and begins to write a short report. The first sign of dawn is beginning to gleam in the dark sky.* STANHOPE *calls " Runner! " as he writes.*

A SOLDIER *comes from the servant's dug-out.*

STANHOPE (*folding the note*): Take this to Battalion Headquarters. There's no reply.

SOLDIER: Yessir.

The SOLDIER *salutes and goes up the steps.*

A plaintive noise comes from the other dug-out. TROTTER *is singing " There's a long, long trail a-winding."* STANHOPE *listens for a moment, then rises, takes a few small coins from his pocket, and throws them into* TROTTER'S *dug-out. The singing stops abruptly. After a moment* TROTTER'S *voice comes.*

TROTTER: Thank you kindly, guv'nor!

The SERGEANT-MAJOR *comes down the steps.*

STANHOPE: Morning, sergeant-major.

S.-M.: Morning, sir. Wiring parties are just in, sir. Made a decent job of it—right down to the support line.

STANHOPE: Good. Everything quiet?

S.-M.: It's all right opposite 'ere, sir, but the guns are goin' 'ard down south. 'Eavy bombardment. Not sure if it ain't spreading up this way, sir.

STANHOPE: Very likely it is. The officers are coming up in a minute. They'll stand by with their platoons. I must stay here awhile in case of messages. I shall come up directly things begin to happen.

S.-M.: Very good, sir.

STANHOPE: Are the men having their tea?

S.-M.: Yessir.

STANHOPE: Let 'em have a decent drop of rum.

S.-M.: About 'arf again, sir?

STANHOPE: Yes.

S.-M.: If the attack don't come, sir, 'ow long are we to stand-to?

STANHOPE: We must expect the attack any time up till midday. After then I don't think it'll come till tomorrow.

S.-M.: Very good, sir.

STANHOPE: We must naturally make our plans to meet things as they happen.

S.-M.: Quite, sir.

STANHOPE: All right, sergeant-major. I'll see you up there soon.

S.-M.: Yessir.

He salutes and goes away.

MASON *brings in four little packets of sandwiches, and puts one packet on the table for* STANHOPE.

MASON: Your sambridges, sir. 'Arf bully beef and 'arf sardine. Sardine on top, sir.

STANHOPE: How delicious. No *pâté de foie gras?*

MASON: No what, sir?

STANHOPE: No *pâté de foie gras?*

MASON: No, sir. The milkman 'asn't been yet.

MASON *takes the other parcels to the left-hand dug-out.*

STANHOPE *pours a little whisky into his tea and the remainder of the contents of the bottle into his flask.*

MASON *returns.*

STANHOPE: Get dressed as soon as you can.

MASON: Yessir.

MASON *goes out.*

TROTTER *comes in, fully dressed for the line.*

TROTTER: All ready, skipper. Want me to go up?

STANHOPE: Yes. I think so. Go right round the line and see everything's all right. I'll be up soon.

Suddenly there comes the faint whistle and thud of falling shells—a few seconds between each. STANHOPE *and* TROTTER *listen intently, four shells fall, then silence.*

TROTTER: 'Ullo, 'ullo.

STANHOPE *strides to the doorway, goes up a few steps, and looks out into the night. He comes slowly back.*

STANHOPE: Over on Lancer's Alley—somewhere by the reserve line.

There comes the louder thud of three more shells.

TROTTER: That's nearer.

STANHOPE: Better go up, Trotter. Call the others.

TROTTER (*at the left-hand dug-out*): 'Ibbert! Raleigh! come on! (*He lights a cigarette over the candle,—lingers a moment, and slowly goes up the steps.*) Cheero, skipper. See you later.

STANHOPE: Send your runner down to tell me how things are going.

TROTTER: Righto.

TROTTER disappears into the dark.

A vague white line of dawn is broadening above the dark trench wall outside. STANHOPE *sits at the table and sips his tea. He takes a cigarette and lights it with a quivering hand.*

RALEIGH *comes from his dug-out.*

STANHOPE *lowers his head and writes in his notebook.*

RALEIGH: Do you want me to go up?

STANHOPE (*without looking up*): Yes. Trotter's gone.

RALEIGH: Right. (*He goes to the steps and turns shyly.*) Cheero—Stanhope.

STANHOPE (*still writing with lowered head*): Cheero, Raleigh. I shall be coming up soon. (RALEIGH *goes up the steps.*)

STANHOPE *stops writing, raises his head, and listens. The shells are falling steadily now. He glances towards the left-hand dug-out and calls:*

Hibbert!

There is no reply. He slowly rises and goes to the left-hand dug-out doorway, he calls again—louder:

Hibbert!! (*He looks into the doorway and says*) What are you doing?

HIBBERT *appears. He is very pale; he moves as if half asleep.*

Come along, man!

HIBBERT: You want me to go up now?

STANHOPE: Of course I do. The others have gone.

HIBBERT: Got a drop of water?

STANHOPE: What d'you want water for?

HIBBERT: I'm so frightfully thirsty. All that champagne and stuff—dried my mouth up.

STANHOPE *pours a drop of water into a mug and gives it to* HIBBERT.

STANHOPE: Here you are. Didn't you have any tea?

HIBBERT: Yes.   It was a bit sweet, though.

The shelling is steadily increasing, and now, above the lighter " crush " of the smaller shells, there comes the deep resounding " boom " of Minenwerfer. HIBBERT *sips his water very slowly, rinsing his mouth deliberately with each sip.* STANHOPE *is by the doorway, looking up into the trench. He has just turned away as a sonorous drawn-out call comes floating through the dawn:* " Stretcher bear-ers! "

STANHOPE *half turns, then faces* HIBBERT.

STANHOPE: Come on.   Buck up.

HIBBERT: There's no appalling hurry, is there?

STANHOPE: No hurry! Why d'you think the others have gone up?

HIBBERT (*slowly*): What? Trotter and Raleigh?

STANHOPE (*sharply*): Wake up, man! What the devil's the matter with you?

HIBBERT *slowly puts down his mug.*

HIBBERT: Champagne dries the mouth up so. Makes the tongue feel like a bit of paper.

There is a slight pause.

STANHOPE: The longer you stay here, the harder it'll be to go up.

HIBBERT: Good Lord! You don't think I'm——

STANHOPE: You're just wasting as much time as you can.

HIBBERT: Well, damn it, it's no good going up till I feel fit. Let's just have another spot of water.

HIBBERT *takes the jug and pours out a little more water. He is the picture of misery.* STANHOPE *stands impatiently beside him.*

MASON *appears from his dug-out, fully dressed for the line, his rifle slung over his shoulder.*

MASON: I'll go right along, sir. I've made up the fire to last a good three hours—if you don't mind me popping down about nine o'clock to 'ave a look at it.

STANHOPE: All right, Mason. Mr. Hibbert's coming up now. You can go along with him.

MASON (*to* HIBBERT): I'd like to come along of you if you don't mind, sir. I ain't bin up in this part of the front line. Don't want to get lorst.

STANHOPE: Mr. Hibbert'll show you the way up. (*He turns to* HIBBERT.) Keep your men against the back wall of the trench as long as the shells are dropping behind. Cheero!

HIBBERT *looks at* STANHOPE *for a moment, then with a slight smile, he goes slowly up the steps and into the trench,* MASON *following behind.*

A dark figure stands out against the pale sky; comes hurrying down the steps—a PRIVATE SOLDIER, *out of breath and excited.*

Yes?

SOLDIER: Message from Mr. Trotter, sir. Shells falling mostly behind support line. Minnies along front line.

STANHOPE: Who's just been hit?

SOLDIER: Corporal Ross, I think it was, sir. Minnie dropped in the trench at the corner—just as I come away.

The SERGEANT-MAJOR *comes down the steps, very much out of breath.*

STANHOPE (*to the* SOLDIER): All right, thanks.

The SOLDIER *salutes, and goes up the steps slower than he came.*

S.-M.: Beginning to get 'ot, sir.

STANHOPE: Corporal Ross hit?

S.-M.: Yessir.

STANHOPE: Badly?

S.-M.: Pretty badly, sir.

STANHOPE: Most of the shelling's going over, isn't it?

S.-M.: Most of the *shells* is be'ind, sir, but there's Minnies and rifle grenades along the front line. Pretty 'ot it's getting, sir. They're attacking down south—there's rifle fire.

STANHOPE: All right, sergeant-major; thanks.

S.-M.: What I come to ask, sir—what about the wounded— getting 'em down, sir? The shelling's pretty thick over Lancer's Alley.

STANHOPE: What about Fosse Way?

S.-M.: Pretty bad there, too, sir.

STANHOPE: Don't try then. Take anyone badly hit down into the big dug-out on the right. Let the stretcher-bearers do what they can there.

S.-M.: Very good, sir.

STANHOPE: Only Corporal Ross hit?

S.-M.: That's all, sir——

Again there comes the drawn-out call—several times as it is passed from man to man: " Stretcher bear-ers! "

The SERGEANT-MAJOR'S *eyes meet* STANHOPE'S. *He turns and goes up the steps.*

STANHOPE *is alone. Flying fragments of shell whistle and hiss and moan overhead. The sharp* " *crack* " *of the rifle grenades, the thud of the shells, and the boom of the Minenwerfer mingle together in a muffled roar.* STANHOPE *takes his belt from the table and buckles it on, puts his revolver lanyard round his neck, and drops his flask and sandwiches into his pocket.*

The SERGEANT-MAJOR *reappears and comes hurrying down the steps.*

STANHOPE (*turning quickly*): What is it, sergeant-major?

S.-M.: Mr. Raleigh, sir——

STANHOPE: What!

S.-M.: Mr. Raleigh's been 'it, sir. Bit of shell's got 'im in the back.

STANHOPE: Badly?

S.-M.: Fraid it's broke 'is spine, sir; can't move 'is legs.

STANHOPE: Bring him down here.

S.-M.: Down 'ere, sir?

STANHOPE (*shouting*): Yes! Down here—quickly!

The SERGEANT-MAJOR *hurries up the steps. A shell screams and bursts very near. The* SERGEANT-MAJOR *shrinks back and throws his hand across his face, as though a human hand could ward off the hot flying pieces. He stumbles on again into the trench, and hurriedly away.*

STANHOPE *is by* OSBORNE'S *bed, fumbling a blanket over it. He takes a trench coat off the wall and rolls it for a pillow. He goes to his own bed, takes up his blanket, and turns as the* SERGEANT-MAJOR *comes carefully down the steps carrying* RALEIGH *like a child in his huge arms.*

(*With blanket ready.*) Lay him down there.

S.-M.: 'E's fainted, sir. 'E was conscious when I picked 'im up.

The SERGEANT-MAJOR *lays the boy gently on the bed; he draws away his hands, looks furtively at the palms, and wipes the blood on the sides of his trousers.* STANHOPE *covers* RALEIGH *with his blanket, looks intently at the boy, and turns to the* SERGEANT-MAJOR.

STANHOPE: Have they dressed the wound?

S.-M.: They've just put a pad on it, sir. Can't do no more.

STANHOPE: Go at once and bring two men with a stretcher.

S.-M.: We'll never get 'im down, sir, with them shells falling on Lancer's Alley.

STANHOPE: Did you hear what I said? Go and get two men with a stretcher.

S.-M. (*after a moment's hesitation*): Very good, sir.

The SERGEANT-MAJOR *goes slowly away.*

STANHOPE *turns to* RALEIGH *once more, then goes to the table, pushes his handkerchief into the water-jug, and brings it, wringing wet, to* RALEIGH'S *bed. He bathes the boy's face. Presently* RALEIGH *gives a little moan, opens his eyes, and turns his head.*

RALEIGH: Hullo—Dennis——

STANHOPE: Well, Jimmy—(*he smiles*)—you got one quickly.

There is silence for a while. STANHOPE *is sitting on a box beside* RALEIGH. *Presently* RALEIGH *speaks again—in a wondering voice.*

RALEIGH: Why—how did I get down here?

STANHOPE: Sergeant-major brought you down.

RALEIGH *speaks again, vaguely, trying to recollect.*

RALEIGH: Something—hit me in the back—knocked me clean over—sort of—winded me—— I'm all right now. (*He tries to rise.*)

STANHOPE: Steady, old boy. Just lie there quietly for a bit.

RALEIGH: I'll be better if I get up and walk about. It happened once before—I got kicked in just the same place at Rugger; it—it soon wore off. It—it just numbs you for a bit. (*There is a pause.*) What's that rumbling noise?

STANHOPE: The guns are making a bit of a row.

RALEIGH: Our guns?

STANHOPE: No. Mostly theirs.

Again there is silence in the dug-out. A very faint rose light is beginning to glow in the dawn sky. RALEIGH *speaks again—uneasily.*

RALEIGH: I say—Dennis——

STANHOPE: Yes, old boy?

RALEIGH: It—it hasn't gone through, has it? It only just hit me?—and knocked me down?

STANHOPE: It's just gone through a bit, Jimmy.

RALEIGH: I won't have to—go on lying here?

STANHOPE: I'm going to have you taken away.

RALEIGH: Away? Where?

STANHOPE: Down to the dressing-station—then hospital—then home. (*He smiles.*) You've got a Blighty one,[1] Jimmy.

RALEIGH: But I—I can't go home just for—for a knock in the back. (*He stirs restlessly.*) I'm certain I'll be better if—if I get up. (*He tries to raise himself, and gives a sudden cry.*) Oh—God! It does hurt!

STANHOPE: It's bound to hurt, Jimmy.

RALEIGH: What's—on my legs? Something holding them down——

STANHOPE: It's all right, old chap; it's just the shock—numbed them.

Again there is a pause. When RALEIGH *speaks, there is a different note in his voice.*

RALEIGH: It's awfully decent of you to bother, Dennis. I feel rotten lying here—everybody else—up there.

[1] Blighty one—Blighty meant England, and a Blighty one was a wound which would require hospital treatment in England. It was considered a piece of luck.

STANHOPE: It's not your fault, Jimmy.

RALEIGH: So—damn—silly—getting hit. (*Pause.*) Is there—just a drop of water?

STANHOPE (*rising quickly*): Sure. I've got some here.

He pours some water into the mug and brings it to RALEIGH.

(*Cheerfully.*) Got some tea-leaves in it. D'you mind?

RALEIGH: No. That's all right—thanks——

STANHOPE holds the mug to RALEIGH's *lips, and the boy drinks.*

I say, Dennis, don't you wait—if—if you want to be getting on.

STANHOPE: It's quite all right, Jimmy.

RALEIGH: Can you stay for a bit?

STANHOPE: Of course I can.

RALEIGH (*faintly*): Thanks awfully.

There is quiet in the dug-out for a long time. STANHOPE *sits with one hand on* RALEIGH's *arm, and* RALEIGH *lies very still. Presently he speaks again—hardly above a whisper.*

Dennis——

STANHOPE: Yes, old boy?

RALEIGH: Could we have a light? It's—it's so frightfully dark and cold.

STANHOPE (*rising*): Sure! I'll bring a candle and get another blanket.

STANHOPE goes to the left-hand dug-out, and RALEIGH *is alone, very still and quiet, on* OSBORNE's *bed. The faint rosy glow of the dawn is deepening to an angry red. The grey night sky is dissolving, and the stars begin to go. A tiny sound comes from where* RALEIGH *is lying—something between a sob and a moan.* STANHOPE *comes back with a blanket. He takes a candle from the table and carries it to* RALEIGH's *bed. He puts it on the box beside* RALEIGH *and speaks cheerfully.*

Is that better, Jimmy? (RALEIGH *makes no sign.*) Jimmy——

Still RALEIGH *is quiet.* STANHOPE *gently takes his hand. There is a long silence.* STANHOPE *lowers* RALEIGH's *hand to the bed, rises, and takes the candle back to the table. He sits on the bench behind the table with his back to the wall, and stares listlessly across at the boy on* OSBORNE'S *bed. The solitary candle-flame throws up the lines on his pale, drawn face, and the dark shadows under his tired eyes. The thudding of the shells rises and falls like an angry sea.*

A PRIVATE SOLDIER *comes scrambling down the steps, his round, red face wet with perspiration, his chest heaving for breath.*

SOLDIER: Message from Mr. Trotter, sir—will you come at once.

STANHOPE *gazes round at the* SOLDIER—*and makes no other sign.*

Mr. Trotter, sir—says will you come at once!

STANHOPE *rises stiffly and takes his helmet from the table.*

STANHOPE: All right, Broughton, I'm coming.

The SOLDIER *turns and goes away.*

STANHOPE *pauses for a moment by* OSBORNE'S *bed and lightly runs his fingers over* RALEIGH'S *tousled hair. He goes stiffly up the steps, his tall figure black against the dawn sky.*

The shelling has risen to a great fury. The solitary candle burns with a steady flame, and RALEIGH *lies in the shadows. The whine of a shell rises to a shriek and bursts on the dug-out roof. The shock stabs out the candle-flame; the timber props of the door cave slowly in, sandbags fall and block the passage to the open air.*

There is darkness in the dug-out. Here and there the red dawn glows through the jagged holes of the broken doorway.

Very faintly there comes the dull rattle of machine-guns and the fevered spatter of rifle fire.

THE PLAY ENDS

QUESTIONS ON *JOURNEY'S END*

DETAILED QUESTIONS ON TEXT

ACT I

1. Show how valuable Hardy is in providing the audience with necessary information and setting the scene.
Collect examples of his kind of humour.

2. Assemble evidence that Hardy is a less conscientious and efficient commanding officer than Stanhope. (Notice, for example, which bed Stanhope chooses.)

3. How does Raleigh reveal that he is young and inexperienced? Find examples of Osborne's tact in helping Raleigh to settle in.

4. Sum up what we have learnt about Stanhope before he first appears.

5. Study the first meeting between Raleigh and Stanhope. Why is it so difficult for them to be at ease together? Notice the part played by Osborne in trying to smooth over the awkwardness.

6. " War's bad enough *with* pepper—but war without pepper —it's—it's bloody awful." Collect other examples of Trotter's ironic joking about the war.

7. In producing the play one would need to divide each act or scene into sub-sections, which might be thought of as movements. Each of these may be intended to tell a bit of the story, to reveal something important about character or to provide light relief. Each section has its own climax. Sections vary in pace or atmosphere. Try to split up Act I into sections and say what is the function or value of each. Which section is the most tense? Which is the quietest and most serene?

ACT II—SCENE 1

8. How does Trotter " make things feel natural "?

9. The quiet talk about gardening and playing for England deepens our understanding of the characters concerned. It provides a contrast between the life these men have left behind and the life they must endure now.

It also sets an atmosphere of calm before the coming storm—another case of contrast.

This storm is over the letter, and it is worth detailed study from the moment when Raleigh goes out to write his letter.

First we must be prepared for Stanhope's outburst. Show how the strain that is afflicting him is explained and developed. Notice the different ways in which Osborne tries to moderate the growing friction. From the moment when Raleigh comes in with his letter the scene rises to a climax. Quarrelling and anger (even when one-sided, as here) are generally dramatic, but notice that the painful quiet at the end is as effective dramatically as the shouting that preceded it.   Why?

10. Draw a diagram, like a graph, to indicate the *shape*, in terms of dramatic tension, of the last three pages of the scene.

ACT II—SCENE 2

11. What further anxieties are shown to be added to the strain that Stanhope has to bear? Notice the ironic joking which keeps emotion in restraint.

12. Describe the *shape* of the scene with the Colonel.

13. How does the scene with Hibbert increase our respect for Stanhope? Examine the *shape* of this scene, watching for the quiet patches as well as the storms.

14. How is the Colonel's plan for the raid received by (a) Osborne; (b) Trotter; (c) Raleigh? How does each of them reveal his character by his reaction?

ACT III—SCENE 1

15. Look at the talk between Osborne and Raleigh before the raid. How does it show that they are nervous? What has the audience already learnt about the danger of the operation?

16. How does the Colonel's attitude to the raid differ from Raleigh's? Is there any implied bitterness here against the higher command or would you be the same if you were the Colonel?

17. Why is Stanhope so brutal to Raleigh after Osborne's death? Which of them are you more sorry for after the outburst?

ACT III—SCENE 2

18. Explain Stanhope's anger at the party with (*a*) Hibbert; (*b*) Raleigh. Notice the contrast.

19. The attack has been expected since the beginning of the play. How is the sense of increasing danger quickened in this scene?

20. Show how the emotion in the last three pages is kept in restraint to avoid sentimentality.

GENERAL QUESTIONS

1. Analyse the dramatic purpose of Mason's entrances and preoccupations.

2. In what respects does Mason resemble Trotter? Why do the nerves of these two remain steady while Hibbert cracks and Stanhope has to depend on whisky?

3. "Think what a dear, level-headed old thing you are," Hardy says to Osborne. Find supporting evidence in the play.

4. One essential of drama is Conflict. (*a*) Show how all the characters, including the German prisoner, are united in conflict with the external forces of war. (*b*) In which scene does the dramatic excitement depend on conflict of wills among the characters?

5. Much of the emotion of the play comes from the relationship between Raleigh and Stanhope, both of whom have the sympathy of the audience. What makes the barrier between them so poignant, and how is it removed in the end?

6. Write about the type of humour which the men use as a means of concealing their real feelings.

7. Estimate the importance of food and talk of food in revealing character.

8. Assuming that Hibbert's neuralgia was genuine, how far do you sympathise with him? At what stage do you despise him most? What is his dramatic value in the play?

9. At which moments is Stanhope most unreasonable? Where do you admire him most? Where do you pity him most?

10. Do you agree with Hardy that Osborne would make a better commanding officer than Stanhope?

11. Here is a poem by Siegfried Sassoon, published in 1918. How much of it is appropriate to the characters in *Journey's End*?

DREAMERS

Soldiers are citizens of death's grey land,
    Drawing no dividend from time's tomorrows.
In the great hour of destiny they stand,
    Each with his feuds, and jealousies, and sorrows.
Soldiers are sworn to action; they must win
    Some flaming, fatal climax with their lives.
Soldiers are dreamers; when the guns begin
    They think of firelit homes, clean beds, and wives.

I see them in foul dug-outs, gnawed by rats,
    And in the ruined trenches, lashed with rain,
Dreaming of things they did with balls and bats,
    And mocked by hopeless longing to regain
Bank-holidays, and picture shows, and spats,
    And going to the office in the train.

from *Counter Attack*.

FURTHER READING

Readers who wish to know more of what the war of 1914–18 was like should try:

The war poems of Siegfried Sassoon and Wilfred Owen.

Sassoon, *Memoirs of an Infantry Officer* (autobiographical novel).

Graves, *Goodbye to All That* (memoirs).

Remarque, *All Quiet on the Western Front* (novel, from the German side).

Blunden, *Undertones of War* (memoirs and poems).

Barbusse, *Under Fire* (a Frenchman's view).

ACKNOWLEDGMENT

The poem "Dreamers" has been reprinted here by kind permission of Mr. Siegfried Sassoon.